THE CODEBREAKERS OF BLETCHLEY PARK

Dermot Turing

Foreword by Christopher Andrew

Picture Credits:

Alamy: 179, 187
Bletchley Park Trust: 13, 46 (Judie Hodsdon), 54, 138, 181 (Judie Hodsdon), 199
Bridgeman Images: 80
Clarke Family: 154
GCHQ: 120, 124
Getty Images: 132, 141, 174, 231
Joel Greenberg: 27 (Denniston Family), 105 (Welchman Family)
Keen Family: 189
King's College, Cambridge: 99
NARA: 36
NSA: 92, 135, 161, 168,
Public Domain: 20, 25, 52, 68, 75, 101, 115, 144, 150, 152, 204, 211, 222
Shutterstock: 72,
Shutterstock Editorial: 226, 241

This edition published in 2020 by Arcturus Publishing Limited
26/27 Bickels Yard, 151–153 Bermondsey Street,
London SE1 3HA

AD006862UK

Printed in the UK

Contents

 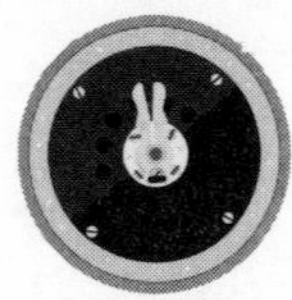 

Foreword

Less than half a century ago, Bletchley Park remained probably the best-kept major secret in British history. Its members, in Churchill's now famous phrase, were 'the geese that laid the golden eggs, but never cackled'. Even at the end of the war, when most returned to civilian life, they were firmly reminded that they must keep their wartime work completely secret for the rest of their lives – even from close family and friends

Bletchley's post-war successor, GCHQ, feared, however, that some of the clues to the wartime ULTRA intelligence derived from breaking Enigma and other high-grade enemy ciphers were too obvious for alert historians of the war to miss. It was common knowledge that British cryptanalysts had broken German ciphers during World War I; indeed one German decrypt – the 1917 'Zimmermann telegram' – had made front-page news on both sides of the Atlantic and may even have hastened American entry into the War.

The published 1945–6 hearings of the Congressional Joint Committee on the Investigation of the Pearl Harbor Attack also revealed in great detail US decryption of Japanese diplomatic telegrams before the attack and the White House's knowledge of them. So it was difficult for GCHQ to understand why, for thirty years, no historian publicly posed the rather obvious question of whether German ciphers had been broken in World War II as well as in World War I.

Most Oxbridge Colleges and many other universities had historians or other academics who had worked at Bletchley and knew the answer to the unasked question. When I first became assistant lecturer at Cambridge in 1967, quite a number were colleagues in the History and neighbouring faculties. *The Codebreakers of Bletchley Park* brings them vividly back to life. Among our friends and neighbours in Newnham were three couples who had met and married at Bletchley Park: Harry and Hilary Hinsley, Christopher and Helen Morris, Patrick and Sydney Wilkinson.

In their lectures and talks before the mid-1970s, when the ULTRA Secret was at last officially acknowledged, none made any reference not merely to Bletchley Park but to any other example of signals intelligence (Sigint), the interception and decryption (if necessary) of signals and other communications. Even the word Sigint remained taboo. When I gave a paper in 1970 to Harry Hinsley's international relations seminar on French codebreaking during the Third Republic, he felt bound to use the formula 'what Christopher Andrew refers to as Sigint', when commenting on it.

When I began teaching a course on intelligence history at Cambridge, I used to remind students that, at their age, some of their World War II predecessors had been working at Bletchley rather than studying for a degree. Harry Hinsley was recruited at the age of twenty after only two years as an undergraduate reading history. Alan Stripp, with whom he later edited the first book of Bletchley reminiscences, was younger still; he was an eighteen year-old first-year classics scholar at Trinity College when recruited as a codebreaker in 1942.

The only previous occasion when such young recruits had a major role in British intelligence was in the reign of Queen Elizabeth I, whose intelligence chief, Sir Francis Walsingham, an alumnus of King's College, Cambridge, recruited a series of talented Cambridge students from his former university – including the twenty-one-year-old Christopher Marlowe in 1585. Probably none of those engaged in breaking Hitler's ciphers at Bletchley Park, knew that Walsingham's main codebreaker, Thomas Phelippes, probably a graduate of Trinity College, broke the ciphers of Philip II of Spain before the Armada (though some of the historians may have known that he broke those of Mary Queen of Scots). Walsingham told Phelippes that he would 'not believe in how good part [the Queen] accepteth of your service'; she awarded him a royal pension.

Gender historians almost invariably ignore intelligence history. They are wrong to do so. The first British government department to break the glass ceiling was MI5 in 1992 when, with the appointment of Stella Rimington as DG, it became the first major intelligence agency anywhere in the world with a female head. As far back as the beginning of World War I, the decision by MI5's then non-graduate male hierarchy to recruit secretarial staff from two Oxford women's colleges, Royal Holloway College (also female) and Cheltenham Ladies' College made MI5 the first official agency with a minority of women who were better educated and from families higher up the social scale than most of their male colleagues.

The list compiled in March 1939 by the first head of Bletchley Park, Alastair Denniston, of 73 academics ('men of the professor type') suitable for wartime work at Bletchley Park included only two women. Though their numbers increased steadily and 75% of Bletchley staff were women by 1945, codebreaking was officially classed as a male occupation. As Sir Dermot Turing shows, female codebreakers had therefore to be given misleading titles such as 'clerical staff' or 'translator'. Some of their talents, such as those of Alison Fairlie, were fully exploited. Those of a number of other female 'translators', however, were not. Miriam Rothschild, later DBE, FRS and one of Britain's leading scientists, seems to have been given limited scope for her remarkable range of talents. Her brother Victor Rothschild, also a future FRS, was given a much more important role in MI5.

Like MI5 and SIS (also known as MI6), Bletchley Park was penetrated by Soviet intelligence – in the person of John Cairncross, the 'Fifth Man' of the Cambridge Five. Cairncross was at Bletchley for only a year and not the only source of Sigint obtained by Soviet intelligence in Britain. But for Frank Birch, one of the most remarkable of the

Codebreakers of Bletchley Park, Soviet penetration would have been far worse. Birch was a veteran World War I codebreaker who returned to Sigint at the outbreak of the Second, after spending most of the 1930s acting on stage and screen. Birch rose to become Deputy Director of GCHQ at the end of the war before returning to acting in 1946.

In 1940 Birch was responsible for interviewing his fellow Cambridge graduate, Kim Philby, a Soviet agent since 1934, who was seeking a job at Bletchley Park. According to Philby, Birch rejected him, despite his fluent German, 'on the infuriating ground that he could not offer enough money to make it worth my while'. Philby's explanation is unconvincing. Very few, if any, of those at Bletchley Park joined because of the salary it offered. It is far more likely that Birch distrusted him. Excluded from Bletchley, Philby, with help from his Cambridge contemporary and fellow Soviet agent, Guy Burgess, found a job in SIS, where, for more than a decade, he provided so much intelligence that Moscow sometimes found difficulty in coping with it. Had Birch admitted him, he would no doubt have tried to do the same at Bletchley Park.

Christopher Andrew

Introduction

When the story of Bletchley Park and its achievements during World War II first reached the public in the mid-1970s, there was remarkably little discussion of the codebreakers who had made the place what it was. Frederick Winterbotham's book, *The Ultra Secret*, sold over four million copies without a single mention of Alan Turing. The first biography of Alan Turing, published in 1959, did not mention Bletchley Park, partly because it was still a secret, but mainly because the biographer, Alan Turing's mother (and my grandmother) had nothing except her own speculations to go on concerning what Bletchley Park had been about and her son's job there.

Slowly, over the next 15 years or so, some of the details of the story were filled in. Documents were released into the National Archives, and it became possible to learn about the operational impact of the intelligence generated by Bletchley Park. Later, the technical breakthroughs which had mechanized codebreaking, leading to a generation of proto-computers, captured the imagination. Yet none of those stories were about the people who populated Bletchley Park. Admittedly, in the earliest days, when there were still restrictions on revealing the technical details, the now-retired codebreakers penned their memoirs and wrote about the eccentric boffins with whom they worked; later on, when the Bletchley Park site itself opened as a museum, the surviving veterans – predominantly the girls and young women who had worked on the machinery at Bletchley and its outstations – had their turn at telling their personal stories.

Those stories have immense value as entertainment, and to get a flavour – literally – of the conditions at Bletchley. 'It took nine months before anything was done about our request not to have the leftovers from the 6 pm dinner served up tepid for our breakfast,' recalled one servicewoman who was accommodated at Woburn Abbey during the latter years of the war. She was doing the night shift, so the tepid breakfast was served in the evening: 'We came down at 10 pm to face steak and kidney pudding which was mostly soggy batter and gravy, with yellow cabbage that smelt of drains.' Many teenage girls were recruited to operate bombe machines at the two large outstations serving Bletchley Park's Enigma-breaking division, located in North London at Eastcote and Stanmore. According to one of the Stanmore girls, 'The food in wartime was never particularly plentiful or of good quality, but at Stanmore it seemed particularly bad. I remember specifically a concoction known as "scented sausages" and I have never smelled anything like it before or since.'

All that was a far cry from the earliest days, when Bletchley Park was first established as a war station for the Secret Intelligence Service (MI6), whose chief is said to have installed his favourite chef from the Savoy Grill in the mansion at Bletchley to keep the first contingent of codebreakers well-fed. That transformation gives a clue to the story of Bletchley Park: it was not a static thing that happened at one moment in history; rather, it was an evolution, from a pre-mechanical academic approach to codebreaking through to a modern, automated, electronic system which needed factory-style management to be effective. Any snapshot, which is an inevitable result of a single person's memories, risks missing this transformation. Working at Bletchley was to be surrounded by builders, management changes, office upheavals, and personnel problems, even to the extent that sometimes the business of codebreaking – and the codebreakers themselves – slipped out of sight.

So, Bletchley Park was a multi-faceted enterprise. Certainly, there were the eccentric boffins, with the prize going to Alan Turing for the largest number of anecdotes about his unconventional behaviour. An

The mansion and gardens at Bletchley Park as they were in the 1930s.

old favourite is one told by my father (Alan's brother) in the mid-1970s. He wrote, 'At Bletchley (where Alan was known as "the Prof"), he used to cycle to and from work and, in the summer, he would wear his civilian gas mask to ward off hay fever. This apparition caused consternation to others on the road. Some would search the skies for enemy aircraft and others would don their gas masks just to be on the safe side.' But then there were the intelligence staff, the translators and linguists, the managers and engineers, the machine operators and many more. There are as many sides to Bletchley as there were roles for the different people working there.

The convention has it that codebreaking was the province of men – famously 'men of the professor type', in the words of Alastair Denniston, the first head of the Government Code and Cypher School (GC&CS), and the man responsible for recruitment in the pre-war build-up of resources. Although by January 1945 75 per cent of the Bletchley staff were women, the perception is that women were in stereotypically gendered roles, as machine-operators, typists and 'inferior' clerical positions. That may be generally true, but as with all generalizations there are mistakes. For one thing, the 'men' of the professor type included a significant number of women, including women professors, such as Alison Fairlie. The professors were not all 'codebreakers' in the strictest sense of the term – they had numerous roles at Bletchley, as interpretation and assessment of decrypts is a non-trivial job, requiring skill, experience, imagination and attention to detail – but that should not rule them out for consideration as 'codebreakers' in a wider sense. Women like Joan Clarke (see pages 152–3, chapter 6) who worked as codebreakers in the narrowest sense, had to be classified as 'translators' or 'clerical staff', because the Civil Service's gendered role-labels had not caught up with the reality of women's occupations. And again, it would be ludicrous to dismiss women and men who served as translators, machine programmers, administrators or operators of checking-machines (who tested the logical validity of possible Enigma machine settings) as 'not real codebreakers' – ludicrous, since it would assume that the only valid methodology for codebreaking is the pencil-and-squared-paper approach of World War I. Bletchley Park broadened the skills needed for codebreaking and intelligence creation, and women as well as men served across all these divisions. They should all be celebrated, for it took all their efforts to create success.

Alison Fairlie (1917–93)

Alison Fairlie joined Bletchley Park in 1942 after completing her doctorate at Oxford University. That in itself was a close-run thing, since she was engaged in research into the French poet Leconte de Lisle in Paris when Germany invaded France in 1940. Her escape was left to the last minute and involved a hair-raising scramble across the country, all the time trying to keep her precious notes and irreplaceable papers safe, despite overcrowded trains where the risk of separation was acute.

Working on Leconte de Lisle stood her in good stead at Bletchley: interpreting the obscurities of his work equipped her with knowledge of abstruse terms unknown to the other linguists, and her effective approach to research was readily adaptable to the technicalities of heat-seeking torpedoes or direction-finding devices cropping up in decrypted naval messages. She was a woman of the professor type.

After Bletchley she was appointed lecturer in French at Cambridge University, reaching the rank of professor in 1972. Rather than teach language for its own sake, her approach was to bring literary criticism to the study of modern languages, which was something of an innovation in postwar university language teaching. Her teaching style was sometimes scary for students, lost for an answer to Fairlie's probing questions and having to endure apparently endless silence while she waited for a response – any response – as the ash on her cigarette lengthened and lengthened. Nonetheless, Fairlie was greatly admired by her students and colleagues, except perhaps those who were the target of her sardonic rhymes about dull and indecisive committee meetings in her college.

The issue of diversity at Bletchley can be overstated, but what remains remarkable is the ability of the organization not just to recruit a wide range of talent, of somewhat unmilitary style, to provide a vital backup service to the military itself, but to retain its informal working methods. In the first days, the professors and their methods held sway, since that was how GC&CS had operated in the interwar period. But when Bletchley developed into a more professional, more businesslike operation there was a danger that the imaginative and unconventional would be chucked away for the sake of military conformity and doing things in the right way. A memo by Frank Birch to all his sub-section leaders, sent less than a week after D-Day, reprimands them for laxity in ordinary office procedures, for vagueness, carelessness and muddle, for delays and other misdemeanours. The fact that Birch was ticking off his people so late in the war suggests that the haphazard and the spontaneous had not been suppressed when Bletchley Park adapted to a new management style.

Indeed, that spirit prevails now at Bletchley's successor organization, GCHQ: 'Our mission is to keep Britain safe. We bring intelligence and technology together to counter increasingly sophisticated threats. GCHQ intelligence helps keep our forces safe, prevents terrorism and crime and protects against cyberattack. It takes all sorts of different people in different roles to help us to do that. Some are linguists; others are mathematicians. Some work in cryptography; others in project management.'[1] That was a lesson learned in the 1940s, from the codebreakers of Bletchley Park.

Frank Birch (1889–1956)

Frank Birch was a man of the theatre. Like so many of the people who came to intelligence, his involvement in it was an accident, and it came so early that his successes on the stage and his secret career intertwined and alternated.

Birch was the son of a banker, who went to Eton and followed the then-traditional move up to King's College, Cambridge, to study history. At King's he met and befriended

1 'About GCHQ', https://www.gchq-careers.co.uk/about-gchq.html

Dilly Knox, and discovered his talents for writing and acting. Forty plays at the Amateur Dramatic Club and the Marlowe Society featured Birch as actor or producer. The question was how to weave the two careers together.

The plunge into World War I added a new dimension. Birch joined the Royal Navy, serving before the mast in various places, including the Dardanelles. Meanwhile, King's College elected him to a fellowship (Birch said this was only because he was understood to be missing, believed killed). The King's connection also led to Birch being recruited for Room 40 in 1916 as an intelligence analyst.

Back at Cambridge, Birch resumed the conflicting roles of Lecturer in History and Man of the Theatre. From 1925 onwards, he produced over 20 plays, acted in a dozen or more, and wrote several himself. His forte, with a shortish, balding physique, was the classic comic roles – the March Hare and Tweedledum in some *Alice* productions, and Widow Twankey in the classic pantomime *Aladdin*.

On the outbreak of World War II he was recalled to duty at Bletchley Park. The style of a theatre producer did not always work well with a team comprising academics, service personnel and junior clerical staff. The fact is that he was a complex and multi-faceted character, described in his King's College obituary notice variously as 'incomparable mimic, ebullient raconteur, generous and enchanting host', 'Prussianly efficient', and a 'Bohemian lover of good living'.

Writing about the codebreakers has been an inspiration and a process of discovery. It would also have been impossible without the help and suggestions of others. To begin with, there were those who shaped the project, including John Turing, Susan Swalwell and Clare Butterfield.

There are many full-length memoirs and contributed chapters written by the codebreakers themselves. Finding a long account by Patrick Wilkinson of his experiences at Bletchley brought the story into three dimensions, adding significantly to the stories told by Peter Calvocoressi, Gordon Welchman, Jimmy Thirsk, Alastair Denniston and Jerry Roberts, and in a collection edited by F.H. Hinsley and Alan Stripp. In recent years, the literature has been enhanced by writers drawing on oral testimony from those who were there and other research, notably the biographies of Welchman and Denniston by Joel Greenberg, and excellent and engaging books by Michael Smith, Marion Hill, Ralph Erskine and Gwendoline Page – all their works have helped bring the codebreakers to life.

At Bletchley Park, Guy Revell made available documents on several veterans from the archival collection there, and Dr David Kenyon's expertise – and his unpublished academic writings on aspects of Bletchley Park – have been valuable, as always. The archivists at Lady Margaret Hall, Oxford, and King's and Girton Colleges, Cambridge, were generous with their time and dug out materials which have never before been published and gave new insights into the Oxbridge contingent of Bletchley's codebreakers. In this respect, particular mention should be made of Karen Lewis, whose insight into the women's roles at Bletchley was not only novel and fascinating but helped shape the direction of the book. To all of them I am most grateful.

CHAPTER 1
The Old Guard

Bletchley Park didn't begin at Bletchley. The origins of wartime codebreaking date from long before the acquisition by MI6 of the Victorian mansion and gardens near Bletchley railway station, which happened only in 1938 in preparation for World War II. Before that, there had been another world war, and it was during that war that the foundations for the codebreaking service at Bletchley were laid.

Winston Churchill's account of World War I, *The World Crisis*, contains this breathless account: 'At the beginning of September, 1914, the German light cruiser *Magdeburg* was wrecked in the Baltic. The body of a drowned German under-officer was picked up by the Russians a few hours later, and clasped in his bosom by arms rigid in death, were the cipher and signal books of the German Navy….'

The truth was a little more prosaic. It seems that when the Russians attacked the *Magdeburg*, the attempt to scuttle the ship and destroy the confidential papers was bungled, so the Russians found the signal book 'in its customary place in the charthouse'. But the gist of Churchill's story was right: the Russians shared their capture with the British, and it was possible with the aid of the code book to read the signals which the German Navy command was sending to its ships.

And here was the essence of it: signalling in wartime in the twentieth century was no longer the business of flag-waving and notes hastily pencilled on scraps of paper. The new medium of communication was radio. Radio enabled contact over vast distances, and its immediacy allowed the commanders to keep right up to the moment with what was

The Admiralty's Old Building in Whitehall, where in Room 40 codebreakers broke naval and diplomatic coded messages in World War I.

happening at the front. For navies in particular, radio revolutionized the methods of command and control. The only snag was that it was broadcast; anyone could listen in. So, codes and ciphers became routine, and the potential for codebreaking also became apparent.

Room 40

The British Admiralty were not slow to spot the need for a radio-monitoring and cryptanalysis service. Stolen code books were all very well but they were an unreliable way to keep up to date with what the

enemy was saying to itself – indeed, it was surprising that the Germans had not changed their codes after the *Magdeburg* incident. At the outbreak of the war, the Royal Navy had only one wireless intercept station, but the Post Office and private individuals were listening in to the Morse code traffic which was filling the airwaves and started sending their material into the Admiralty. Something needed to be done – and so, in true Senior Service fashion, it was, over lunch. Rear Admiral Henry Oliver (later Sir Henry), Director of Naval Intelligence, met with Alfred Ewing (later Sir Alfred), a distinguished professor of physics who was at the time serving as Director of Naval Education. It occurred to Oliver that during wartime not a lot of educating would be going on, and that Ewing might be better deployed onto unravelling the encrypted wireless messages.

Ewing rapidly realized that he would need a staff, and he gathered up men from around the Naval establishment. Foremost among these was Alastair Denniston (see pages 117–18, chapter 5), who was teaching German to naval cadets at Osborne on the Isle of Wight. When Ewing realized he would need somewhere for the staff to work he was allocated Room 40 in the Admiralty's Old Building. (The New Building has the rather splendid archway over the Mall. The archway rooms are nostalgically associated with Churchill's periods of office as First Lord of the Admiralty, though his official residence was down the road at Admiralty House.)

Jutland

Room 40 was soon on top of the German Navy's movements: although the picture was rarely complete, a good indication of whether the German High Seas Fleet was on the move could be obtained. This information could then be relayed to Sir John Jellicoe, the Admiral commanding the British Grand Fleet at Scapa Flow – and then the Grand Fleet could lure the Germans into a trap, repeating the glorious days of Nelson's victories of the century before.

A case in point is the Battle of Jutland, which began on 31 May 1916. A flurry of coded messages emanating from Germany indicated that the German Fleet was in a high state of readiness and Jellicoe was warned that the Germans would sail early on 31 May. He was instructed to proceed to a position east of Aberdeen and await developments, and Admiral Beatty, leading the battlecruiser fleet from Rosyth, was also heading out to sea. Room 40 had set the trap – it was now for the Grand Fleet to spring it.

Unfortunately, the conversion of raw data into valid intelligence was still in its infancy and things started to unravel. Captain Thomas Jackson,

Director of Naval Operations, visited Room 40 just before noon on 31 May, asking about the location of 'Call sign DK'. What he wanted to know, really, was the location of the German fleet, commanded by Admiral Scheer, which typically used this call sign but on the eve of major operations typically switched to something else. Call sign DK was still in Wilhelmshaven, the German Fleet's home port – but Room 40 staff knew better than to question the irascible Jackson why he was asking. Jackson promptly told Jellicoe that Scheer was not at sea, which delayed Jellicoe's dispositions, gave an unnecessary advantage to the Germans, and caused huge distress in Room 40 at the misuse of their product.

Worse was to come. Admiral Scheer was leading the German squadron of battlecruisers, and had run into the British fleet. However, recognizing he was heavily outnumbered, Scheer prudently decided to turn and sail for home. It was still possible for Jellicoe to catch his prey – provided he could see what was going on. Over the vast space of the North Sea, his eyes and ears were provided by Room 40, who had got a good picture throughout the evening of 31 May – only there were delays and errors and only a partial view got through to Jellicoe. Later, he complained that he had been fed bits and pieces, too little, too late, and the consequence was that Scheer escaped his pincers. But Room 40 had done a job to be proud of.

Blinker Hall

Shortly after the Battle of Jutland, Sir Alfred Ewing had gone. He had been invited to become Principal of the University of Edinburgh. It made sense for him to move on, since it was clear that a new approach to injecting the product of Room 40 into the bloodstream of naval intelligence was needed. In fact, the real head of Room 40 during Ewing's tenure had been Commander Herbert Hope, who liaised between the codebreakers and the naval brass, providing an interpretation of the intelligence in a form which the Sea Lords could understand. By 1917, however, Hope had also been promoted to Captain and given a ship, and so Room 40 had come directly under the control of Captain (later Admiral Sir) Reginald Hall.

Hall was born into the business: his father was the first Director of Naval Intelligence. But Hall had seawater in his veins, and intelligence was not the ideal career for an aspiring young officer. So, a sea officer he was. Hall was promoted rapidly, being made Captain at the age of 35, which indicated that Hall was destined for great things. His battlecruiser HMS *Queen Mary* was part of the squadron sent out to engage the Germans in the Heligoland Bight in August 1914. Three German cruisers and a destroyer were sunk with no British warships lost – a rare example of a clear battle success for the Royal Navy in World War I. Yet what ought to have laid the foundation for a glorious career at sea for Hall led only to the acknowledgement that his health was unequal to the task. A problem with his lungs was exacerbated by the cold and damp at Scapa Flow, and when the position of Director of Naval Intelligence became vacant in the autumn of 1914 Hall took the job. Unlike most traditional navy personnel, he did not see intelligence as a backwater, but as an opportunity to make his mark.

Sir Reginald Hall (1870–1943)

Hall's achievements – most notably with the Zimmermann Telegram – came about because he did not see the need for boundaries to 'naval' intelligence. He added 'Room 45' to Room 40: this would be where coded diplomatic messages would be unravelled. Hall also established relations with MI1(b), ensuring that his more junior staff avoided duplication of effort and sharing material of common interest.

As well as codebreaking, Hall's intelligence network involved him in intrigues and deception plans which are the

Admiral Sir Reginald Hall, the leader of Room 40.

stuff of classic spy novels. He created deception plans whereby false information was fed to the Germans (in coded British messages when Hall knew the Germans had broken the British codes) to lure U-boats to destruction, and a John Buchan-style plot to entrap the German Naval saboteur Captain von Rintelen (self-styled 'the Dark Invader') who was planting bombs in dockyards and ships in America. He is also said to have encountered the spy and femme fatale Mata Hari, whom he described as a 'fat old hag without attraction'. After the war, Hall left the Admiralty to become a Conservative MP, and helped organize the effort against the General Strike in 1926.

As a man, Hall was shortish with piercing blue eyes, and as a senior naval officer, he stood no nonsense but inspired great loyalty and affection in his people. He could have volcanic outbursts of temper, but the eruptions were short and rapidly forgiven. He also had a sense of humour, right to the end: his final days were spent at Claridge's Hotel, where all staff were required to dress in sober black suit, white shirt and black tie. When a plumber came to fix some minor problem, Hall was heard to say, 'If you're the undertaker, my man, you're too early'.

By the time Ewing went to Edinburgh, Hall had got Captain William James doing the former jobs of both Ewing and Hope in Room 40. Hall was nicknamed 'Blinker' because he blinked a lot; James was nicknamed 'Bubbles' because, as a child, he had sat for Sir John Millais, whose painting of that name became famous as an advertisement for Pears' soap. From the records, though, it seems highly unlikely that the codebreakers, however unruly they were, would dare use these names.

The staff inherited from Ewing were rather stretched. In the early days of Room 40, a log book had been maintained into which decoded messages were entered, and then copies were sent out to the people who mattered, such as the Director of Naval Intelligence. But messages which were in unknown codes or which couldn't be dealt with were stuffed into a tin marked 'NSL' which stood for 'not sent in, logged'. 'Truly,' wrote Alastair Denniston, 'NSL only meant "neither sent or logged".' The NSL tin was overflowing and something needed to be done.

Hall recognized the need for an increase in the number of staff. A recruitment drive was initiated – with many new, younger, faces coming from academia. From an establishment of nine clerks in December 1915, the team had grown by December of the following year to 'one confidential writer', plus 15 male and – an innovative step – 20 female clerks. 'Room 40' also needed more rooms. It was officially now called 'ID25' (Intelligence Division 25), clearly showing its place in Hall's hierarchy, and several additional offices were taken over. Although the

Alastair Denniston, who became head of the Government Code and Cypher School, in naval uniform in about 1918.

doors were marked 'No Admittance. Ring Bell' none of the doors actually had a bell. The contradictions of secret intelligence had an Alice in Wonderland quality, something which was not lost on its employees, some of whom had stepped straight out of the pages of Lewis Carroll.

A fertile source of recruits was King's College, Cambridge, from where Hall chose Frank Adcock, Frank Birch and Dilly Knox (see pages 70–73, Chapter 3). Knox was undoubtedly one of the best recruits. His research at Cambridge was on a minor Greek poet, Herodas, who had written scurrilous verse known as Mimes in a bizarre postmodern style. Knox's work was to piece together tiny fragments of papyrus on which the remnants of Herodas' writing had survived; Herodas' style did not make this easy. In fact, it was perfect training for re-assembling code books from bits and pieces of intercepted foreign messages. Knox joined the Room 40 team in 1916, and was put to work on the German flag officers' code, which included code-groups for words or parts of words.

Sir Frank Adcock (1886–1968)

Frank Adcock might not have been an obvious fit for King's College, Cambridge, when he arrived in 1905. The college had more than its fair share of Old Etonians, for whom the Leicestershire-born 'northerner', with an accent to match, seemed out of place. But Adcock was brilliant, and on graduation he was encouraged to go and study with the leading scholar in his field, Professor Ulrich von Wilamowitz-Moellendorff, a classical philologist in Berlin.

After serving in Room 40 during World War I, Adcock returned to academia. He specialized in ancient history; yet, with a picture of Admiral Hall in his rooms, Adcock had not forgotten about Room 40. His gift for making friends with the men about the College, and his perceptiveness in sizing them up, made him a valuable assessor for the College's fellowship elections – and also for the recruitment drive for Bletchley Park. He was knighted in 1954 – though for his work on the Cambridge Ancient History, which may not have been his most important service to his country.

Adcock was probably unaware that his former teacher von Wilamowitz-Moellendorff had a nephew, Georg, who served as a U-boat captain in World War II. U-459 was a type XIV tanker which endured a relentless attack from British aircraft in the Bay of Biscay on 24 July 1943. The loss of U-459 was part of a concerted attack on U-tankers which the German Navy needed to sustain the long-distance operations of the U-boat fleet. The campaign against the tankers was in part successful because both attack U-boats and tankers could be targeted at their rendezvous locations, known through Enigma messages. Those Enigma messages were revealed because of the technology developed by one of Adcock's recruits to Bletchley Park, a mathematician called Alan Turing.

Knox recognized not only that some of these groups stood for the common German word-ending '-en' but that one rather unusual message seemed to have lots of -en groups arranged in a syllabic pattern – and to Knox a pattern of syllables implied poetry, and in this particular case a metric pattern known as dactyls. Knox went up the corridor to where the German-language professors sat, and sure enough the poem was identified as a chunk of Friedrich von Schiller learned by all good school children: '*Ehret die Frauen: sie flechten und weben/Himmliche Rosen im redliche Leben*'.

This roughly means, 'Honour to women: they plait and weave heavenly roses into earthly life' (it's better in German). By filling in the blanks, the professors of Room 40, led by Knox, had untangled a substantial part of the code book which was being used to send heavenly messages about U-boat attacks on British merchant shipping.

It wasn't just codebreakers that were needed, but people who could translate and interpret what the coded messages meant. Different skills, for different jobs. W.F. Clarke, a barrister who wanted to go to sea on the outbreak of war, found himself in Room 40 because he spoke German and somehow Hall had found out about him. Clarke listed four individuals as 'expert cryptographers, Knox being by far the best. The others did various jobs; Birch a trained historian had charge of the section which collected and collated information, my job was Intelligence'. The other three expert cryptographers were Adcock, Nigel de Grey and Lord Lytton, whose sister was a suffragette and who himself later became Viceroy of India.

W.F. (Nobby) Clarke (1883–1961)

If your name was Clarke, in the first half of the twentieth century you were bound to be nicknamed 'Nobby', apparently because nineteenth-century clerks dressed to impress and looked, therefore, like nobs. W.F. Clarke was a barrister by profession, before World War I, so presumably looked the part anyway, and had to endure the nickname.

On the outbreak of war he wanted to join the navy but his eyesight let him down, and after a period as a naval paymaster he was detailed to join Room 40 for a job which, then, was wholly unknown to him. As things transpired, he stayed in codebreaking for 30 years.

On the conclusion of World War I he co-wrote the history of Room 40 with Frank Birch, and then took the role of censor on behalf of the Admiralty, weeding out inappropriate references to signals intelligence from the memoirs of naval officers, and issuing a reprimand to none other than Alfred Ewing, Room 40's erstwhile chief. With the establishment of the Government Code and Cypher School he became head of the Naval Section, its first service-facing section, in 1924.

He tried to help GC&CS prepare for World War II, vigorously combatting the prevailing Admiralty view that the introduction of machine ciphers would defeat the codebreakers. He was proved right, but in the event his own skills were overtaken by the world of machines used for cryptanalysis. Birch took over as head of the Naval Section in 1940, and in his last years in office Clarke found more joy in writing acid sketches of his colleagues, present and past, than in the puzzles of modern codebreaking.

Hall had taken a year or so to fill out his role as Director of Naval Intelligence; by 1917 he was thoroughly in control of what he saw as a full-service intelligence bureau, not confined to naval matters or codebreaking. Codebreaking was certainly part of it, as everything which went by wireless came into the hands of Room 40, but spying, deception and, when possible, international skulduggery were all part of Hall's daily diet.

As a senior naval officer, Hall himself was no pushover. But occasionally, Hall would meet his match. There was an occasion when Winston Churchill, the First Sea Lord, sent for Hall late at night to discuss some new scheme of his. Churchill was opinionated and argumentative, and deployed the full force of his rhetoric on Hall, who was exhausted but unpersuaded. 'I distinctly recall the odd feeling that although it would be wholly against my will, I should in a very short space of time be agreeing with everything he said. But a bit of me rebelled, and … I began to mutter to myself "My name is Hall, my name is Hall".' Churchill asked what Hall was muttering about: 'I told him, "that my name is Hall because if I listen to you much longer I shall be convinced it's Brown."' Churchill got the point that Hall disagreed with his plan, the matter was dropped, and Hall was allowed to go home to bed.

Nigel de Grey (1886–1951)

Like many of the early generation of twentieth-century codebreakers, Nigel de Grey was educated at Eton, but unlike most of them he did not go to university. He tried for the Diplomatic Corps, but having failed to get in he worked for the publisher Heinemann, joining in 1907. De Grey wrote well, with a clarity and lightness of touch which made him perfectly suited to the role. When World War I began he joined the Royal Naval Air Squadron in the Balloon Corps, carrying out observations of the enemy, and getting mentioned in despatches.

He was picked out of the front line to join Room 40 in 1915, rapidly becoming one of the foremost codebreakers of his generation. He had an uncanny skill at guessing the meaning of code-groups which unlocked the meanings of others, seeing patterns and extrapolations which filled out the knowledge of the enemy's entire code-book. The Zimmermann Telegram was de Grey's apogee as a codebreaker, but should be recognized as just one of a catalogue of codebreaking successes. He was quiet, small, thin and modest, but endowed with a fierce intellect and presence which shows that the epithet 'the Dormouse' given to him in *Alice in ID25* was a piece of irony.

After World War I, de Grey returned to publishing, this time as director of the Medici Society. The Society – located in Cork Street, by coincidence the same street as MI1(b)'s wartime home – ran a fine art gallery and published prints, and occasionally issued other publications on artistic matters. This suited de Grey perfectly: he was not just a writer but an actor and painter as well. Artistic skills run in the family, as his younger son Roger was a famous landscape painter, who became President of the Royal Academy and received a knighthood.

When World War II began, de Grey was recalled along with other Room 40 veterans; he was allocated to work on Italian naval codes. De Grey's role at Bletchley was, however, mainly a management one. Bridging the gap between administration and front line codebreaking, Nigel de Grey rode out the various administrative storms which periodically afflicted Bletchley Park, working as Deputy Director. Described by one codebreaker as 'the Mikado', de Grey could terrify younger staff through nothing more sinister than seniority and cool gravity. After the war he stayed on at GCHQ, where he wrote a valuable multi-volume history of *Allied Signals Intelligence Policy and Organization*, which in his measured and lucid style explains a great deal of the early work on Enigma, the relations between Britain and her allies, and how the story of Bletchley Park began.

The Zimmermann Telegram

Hall also wanted to expand the scope, as well as the volume, of what Room 40 could achieve. Apart from the occasional forays of the German High Seas Fleet, the reason why the volume of material being analysed by Room 40 was so large was that the service had taken on the job of monitoring all wireless signals traffic, regardless of its origin. Without disregarding naval signals, Room 40 was operating an entire section dealing with diplomatic communications, and that came into its own in 1917.

In early 1917 Germany decided to step up the submarine war, to include attacks on American ships. Despite the policy of neutrality adopted by America's President Wilson, there was a real danger to Germany that this step would bring the United States into the war on the Allied side. In late 1916, Arthur Zimmermann joined the German Government as foreign minister, and he thought he could see a way through this conundrum: to get Mexico into the war on the German side, and thereby tie down the Americans on their side of the Atlantic. Zimmermann got to work on a telegram.

Zimmermann had not reckoned on Hall, Knox and de Grey. Knox and de Grey had begun the laborious task of trying to reconstruct a new diplomatic code introduced about the time Zimmermann took office, in which Berlin was sending secret communications to Washington. The communications route was unfortunate, in several ways. One was that President Wilson had left the route open to facilitate peace overtures: Berlin and Washington should keep on talking, and if that meant allowing Berlin to send encoded messages via the State Department to the German Embassy that was reasonable enough. The other piece of misfortune was that the British had cut many of the transatlantic cables at the start of the war, and now controlled at least one of the remaining channels through which the Berlin-Washington link passed. That happened to be a radio relay station at Porthcurno in Cornwall, where Admiral Hall took copies of everything passing through. That was, perhaps, an ungentlemanly thing to do, since diplomatic traffic going to Washington ought to remain a secret between friends. But once Knox and de Grey had started to discern that the messages were German-to-German and saw what they were about they recognized they had in their hands something which could change the entire course of the war.

It took a bit of interpolation, but the partial decode which de Grey presented to Hall implied that Zimmermann was offering Mexico a deal: invade the United States, and Germany will ensure that the states of Arizona, New Mexico and Texas were returned to Mexican sovereignty in the postwar peace settlement. The message was dynamite, but in its present form it was unconvincing, and there was no way to show it to the Americans without revealing that the British were reading their mail.

Hall figured out a plan. The message had been relayed again, from the German embassy in Washington to the embassy in Mexico. In Mexico, the Germans did not yet use the new code which Knox and de Grey had been disentangling, but an older one which was much better understood in Room 40. By deploying some of that skulduggery, Hall 'acquired' a copy of the telegram sent to Mexico – not only could this be read completely, confirming the British suspicions, but this version did not suggest anything untoward about the British eavesdropping at Porthcurno. So, within a month of the original discovery in Room 40, the British Foreign Secretary Arthur Balfour presented the American Ambassador with a copy of Nigel de Grey's full decode of the Mexican message. The Americans drew their own conclusions. By this stage, unrestricted submarine warfare had commenced, diplomatic relations between America and Germany had been severed, and now it turned out that Germany was trying to foment a new war between the United States and Mexico. Worse, and perhaps worst of all, was the effrontery of using the peace channel to damage the interests of the United States. The timetable tells the next steps of the story:

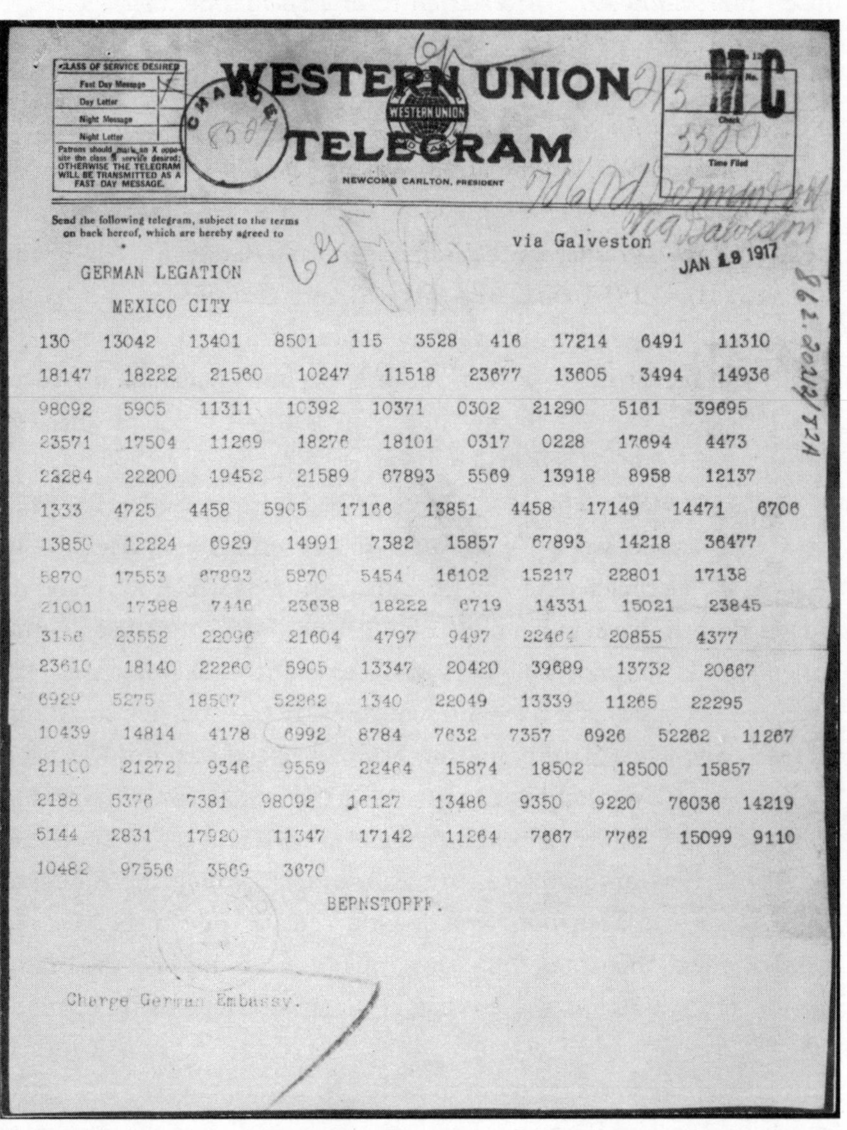

CLASS OF SERVICE DESIRED
Fast Day Message
Day Letter
Night Message
Night Letter
Patrons should mark an X opposite the class of service desired; OTHERWISE THE TELEGRAM WILL BE TRANSMITTED AS A FAST DAY MESSAGE.

WESTERN UNION
TELEGRAM
NEWCOMB CARLTON, PRESIDENT

Send the following telegram, subject to the terms on back hereof, which are hereby agreed to

via Galveston

JAN 19 1917

GERMAN LEGATION

MEXICO CITY

130 13042 13401 8501 115 3528 416 17214 6491 11310
18147 18222 21560 10247 11518 23677 13605 3494 14936
98092 5905 11311 10392 10371 0302 21290 5161 39695
23571 17504 11269 18276 18101 0317 0228 17694 4473
22284 22200 19452 21589 67893 5569 13918 8958 12137
1333 4725 4458 5905 17166 13851 4458 17149 14471 6706
13850 12224 6929 14991 7382 15857 67893 14218 36477
5870 17553 67893 5870 5454 16102 15217 22801 17138
21001 17388 7446 23638 18222 6719 14331 15021 23845
3156 23552 22096 21604 4797 9497 22464 20855 4377
23610 18140 22260 5905 13347 20420 39689 13732 20667
6929 5275 18507 52262 1340 22049 13339 11265 22295
10439 14814 4178 6992 8784 7632 7357 6926 52262 11267
21100 21272 9346 9559 22464 15874 18502 18500 15857
2188 5376 7381 98092 16127 13486 9350 9220 76036 14219
5144 2831 17920 11347 17142 11264 7667 7762 15099 9110
10482 97556 3569 3670

BERNSTORFF.

Charge German Embassy.

The Zimmermann Telegram: when broken by Room 40, its contents shocked America. into declaring war on Germany in 1917

31 January 1917: Germany launches unrestricted submarine warfare.

3 February 1917: America breaks off diplomatic relations with Germany.

23 February 1917: Balfour hands the Zimmermann Telegram to the American Ambassador.

1 March 1917: The text of the telegram is published in American newspapers.

6 April 1917: Congress declares war on Germany.

27 April 1917: Hall promoted to Rear Admiral.

As a final chapter in the story, Admiral Hall was knighted later that same year.

The sailor in Room 53

Knox had settled well into the growing organization called Room 40. One of his preferences was to think in the bath. Unimaginable in today's Civil Service, according to one Room 40 witness a bath-tub was installed for him in Room 53 of the Old Building. Knox had soon annexed Room 53 as a sort of outpost of Room 40. The tale is told that one day, when Knox was reported missing, he was found in deep contemplation over a difficult problem in the steam-filled Room 53, waiting for the bath to fill. Unfortunately, he had omitted to put in the plug. In an end-of-term parody of *Alice's Adventures in Wonderland*, penned by Frank Birch (with some assistance from Knox himself) at the end of the war, there is a piece of poetry. It's not up to the standards of Schiller, or even Herodas, but it contains the following stanza:

The sailor in Room 53
Has never, it's true, been to sea.
But though not in a boat
He has yet served afloat –
In a bath at the Admiralty.

Use of the bath required some sensitivity, since the expansion of Room 40's establishment had led to the hiring of those 20 female clerks. In a rather acid set of recollections from 1951 of his time in the service of Room 40, W.F. Clarke noted:

> *The first entrant was a secretary for [Commander Hope] who only lasted two days when she departed in tears, to be succeeded by the excellent Miss Tribe, who carried on after the war.... The next arrivals were University graduates.... Mrs Bailey ... rather upset things with her love affairs.... Lady Hambro also came, as efficient as her husband must have been in the City; she startled Hope at one of our annual dinners by smoking a very large cigar. I must not forget Miss Curtis, who was in my view the most useful of them all and whom luckily stayed with us until her health broke down in 1944....*

Clarke also mentions 'a small number ... from the universities'. These included 'Miss Nugent, Miss O'Connor, Miss Welsford and Miss May Jenkin who now holds an important position in the BBC.' Also among the female staff was Miss Henderson, daughter of an Admiral; we know that she worked on Italian codes, indicating that the word 'clerk' stood as cover for all kinds of roles.

In addition to the upsetting Mrs Bailey, having women in the team made impressions on the men, who largely came from cloistered backgrounds. Awkwardly, particularly when it came to bathing, the women's shifts were based around office hours, whereas the men working on codes worked naval watches on a 24-hour system. It suddenly seemed rather important to juggle the timetable, in order to ensure things were shipshape and squared away before embarrassment could be caused. Maybe this was managed well; in any event, Dilly Knox fell in love with his secretary Olive Roddam, and his marriage to her was only one of a clutch of Room 40 romances. The tale of Knox's bathing habits even runs to the extent of Olive 'sharing his somewhat bizarre office': one assumes there were desks as well as a tub. Frank Birch also met his wife Vera Gage in Room 40, and Alastair Denniston was another codebreaker whose wife Dorothy Gilliat was a Room 40 alumna.

The postwar period

With the cessation of hostilities there was a risk that Room 40 might not just be downsized but actually disappear altogether. It was at this point that Alastair Denniston emerges from the shadows. Denniston had not had a spectacular success like Knox and de Grey during the war, but as the earliest to join he had seniority; and it was probably for that reason he was selected to join Admiral Beatty as interpreter to accept the surrender of the German Fleet on 21 November 1918. (The Germans did not consider it a 'surrender', and scuttled their interned fleet six months later.)

Shortly after, the other luminaries of Room 40 drifted back to peacetime occupations: Adcock and Birch back to Cambridge, where Knox had been appointed librarian at King's and was soon expected to join them. Birch set to work writing a history of the war at sea from the perspective of the codebreakers, which is closer to Herodas in style than is normal for an official report. (Even more irreverently, there was also a parody of *Alice's Adventures in Wonderland*, called *Alice in ID25*, featuring Hall, Adcock, Denniston, de Grey, Knox and others, with cartoons to match.) Nigel de Grey also took up a new role as director of the Medici Society in London. Denniston stayed on.

By May 1919 there was a serious proposal to establish something mysteriously named a 'Government Code and Cypher School', which, when deciphered, meant a peacetime codebreaking establishment. So far, so good; but inter-service rivalry now crept into the equation. Room 40 may have been hugely successful, but it had not been the only codebreaking effort: Military Intelligence section 1(b) had also broken military codes, working primarily on intercepts obtained through wire-tapping and on front-line communications passing through the mire of the Western Front. It may not have had the glorious coup of the

Zimmermann Telegram, but MI1(b) had had its successes. It had been monitoring diplomatic traffic (while Room 40 focused on German material, MI1(b) looked at everyone else), and after Hall took over Room 40 there had been good cooperation between the two agencies. But the head of MI1(b) did not get on well with Alastair Denniston, even if Denniston had good relations with the mid-grade codebreakers in MI1(b). A new battle was on, as to whether the GC&CS would be a reincarnation of Room 40 or of MI1(b). The services dug in.

While MI1(b) contended for their own priority, failing which their candidate for leader would be withdrawn, Denniston indicated he would be happy to serve in whatever capacity was considered appropriate. His emollience, combined with an artillery shot from Churchill ('Denniston is not only the best man we have had, but he is the only one we have left with special genius for this work'), now restored to the Admiralty as part of the peace process, carried the day. Denniston was going to run the new organization.

The GC&CS was officially established on 1 November 1919. Denniston hired his team from both Room 40 and MI1(b): Knox, of course, and, notably, among those from MI1(b), Oliver Strachey. Strachey, brother of the better-known and more flamboyant Lytton, was on the fringes of the Bloomsbury set, where he met not only Dilly Knox (a friend of Lytton's, and with whom Lytton had fallen into unrequited love) but also his wife Ray Costelloe, who was (like Strachey's mother) an advocate of women's suffrage, a Newnham College mathematics graduate, a painter, parliamentary secretary to Lady Astor (Britain's first woman MP) and the sister-in-law of Virginia Woolf. (Ray went on to become the talent scout for codebreaker women from Newnham, when Bletchley Park needed a recruitment boost.)

Strachey's background as a railway administrator in India might not have been the obvious foundation for a codebreaking career, but the unemployed Oliver – aged 40 at the outbreak of World War I – was introduced through family connections to the War Office and found himself in MI1(b). Strachey was probably the leading cryptanalyst in MI1(b), mastering the breaking of hand-ciphers in which military intelligence specialized. In 1916, he was sent to Egypt, the command centre for the Middle East, which was becoming a key theatre of war. There his job was to inject some good-humoured rigour into the local operation, in order to attack Turkish codes and glean intelligence not just about military plans but the political unrest which was accompanying the break-up of the Ottoman Empire. On his way home, Strachey's ship was torpedoed by a U-boat, an experience he described as an 'inconvenience'.

Now, although outnumbered in the naval and diplomatic takeover of codebreaking by Room 40, Strachey adapted to the new management and mores of the GC&CS. The 'School' had two functions. The publicly admitted one was to advise on the security of codes and ciphers used by the Government. The undercover one was 'to study the methods of cipher communications used by foreign powers'. GC&CS spent its first days monitoring the goings-on behind the scenes of the various peace conferences and treaty negotiations which followed World War I. This, together with the almost complete absence of any signals intelligence relating to the armed forces, led to GC&CS being formally transferred from the Admiralty to the Foreign Office, while reporting to the head of the Secret Intelligence Service (MI6). During the interwar years, Denniston's team broke the codes of all major powers: American, French, German and Japanese, and a sackful of other countries' as well. But, as Denniston himself said, 'the only real operational intelligence came from our work on the Soviet traffic'.

Oliver Strachey (1874–1960)

The Strachey family is best known for the flamboyant Lytton, biographer of Queen Victoria, member of the Bloomsbury

Group, and Cambridge Apostle. Oliver was Lytton's older brother, and was in some ways a contrast to his more extrovert sibling. Oliver went to Eton; Lytton did not. Oliver had a failed term at Balliol College, Oxford, whereas Lytton had a sparkling academic undergraduate career at Cambridge. And Lytton was overtly gay, while Oliver was undeniably hetero.

Before World War I, Strachey was sent to Vienna to develop his talent as a pianist. While there, he perfected his German, which would prove highly valuable in years to come. Strachey was also a friend of Benjamin Britten, with whom he played piano duets.

On the outbreak of World War II, Strachey was still in post at GC&CS. Some say he was the oldest codebreaker at Bletchley Park, but age did not imply any diminution of effectiveness. He continued to work on hand ciphers, in particular those used by the Abwehr, the German military intelligence and counter-intelligence organization. The intelligence derived from this work was called 'ISOS', standing for Illicit Services Oliver Strachey, because the Abwehr agents using the ciphers in question were typically German spies trying to infiltrate the British system in various ways. ISOS provided vital insight into the espionage efforts of the Germans. Armed with ISOS intelligence, the famous 'Double Cross Committee' of the British Security Service tracked down and either locked up or 'turned' every single spy targeted at Britain. He ended the war with a CBE.

Proof of this, but with admittedly mixed results, was the Arcos raid of 1927. As dawn raids go, it was a bit of a flop. The All-Russian Co-operative Society, or Arcos, was notionally a Russian trade agency. In reality, it was a front for Soviet espionage, able to use its specially-negotiated diplomatic status as a cover for its activities. When the British Government decided that Arcos' activities had become too destabilizing, the Home Secretary authorized a raid on its premises for 4.30 am on 12 May 1927. Unfortunately, the operation was badly executed, the main result being a breach in Anglo-Soviet relations. Hastily the British Government tried to excuse itself – by citing GC&CS decrypts to show what the Russians were really up to. But it was a black day for GC&CS: the disclosure that Britain could read encrypted Soviet messages showed the Russians, and all other nations – hostile or otherwise – that Britain was indeed watching them.

In the coming years the degree of sophistication adopted by every country and its armed services for encryption of secret messages continued to advance. Denniston described 1919 as the 'era of bow-and-arrow methods'; by the 1930s machines were being used for encipherment, and a new, modern approach to codebreaking was needed. By 1937, the head of MI6 had decided that another war was inescapable and that GC&CS should begin a recruitment drive.

The Government Code and Cypher School was training for another world war.

CHAPTER 2
The King's High Table

Britain was slow to wake up to the threat posed by Nazi Germany. It was not until 1937 that the Secret Intelligence Service shifted its focus away from Bolshevik Russia to Germany, and there was a continuing official distaste for involvement in European entanglements. Nevertheless, in mid-1937 the head of the Service, Admiral Hugh Sinclair, started to make preparations for a possible conflict with Germany. First of all, there was to be a closer liaison with French Intelligence, particularly on difficult problems like that of the Enigma machine, which the German armed forces were now using to encipher their radio messages. Then there was the question of establishment: an out-of-town location with good communications, and an expansion of staff. Alastair Denniston was instructed to build a list of suitable personnel to cope with the expected increase in demand for codebreaking if indeed the worst came to the worst. And a search began for a suitable set of premises.

A large estate with mansion house, outbuildings and gardens had come onto the market. The estate was conveniently situated: good rail and road links to London, but not too close in case of bombing raids; and, most importantly, within a mile or so of the major telecommunications infrastructure leading north out of London. The place was called Bletchley Park, and the nearest town was Bletchley, which was somewhat nondescript, having built up around the railway junction situated there. It would do perfectly. The grounds provided space for expansion and the anonymity of the location, coupled with the communications links, would enable secret work to be carried on

MI6 acquired Bletchley Park in 1938, and shortly afterwards a group of spies and codebreakers assembled there under the guise of 'Captain Ridley's shooting party'.

while the codebreakers remained in close touch with the consumers of their product. Sinclair bought the house and grounds for the service in June 1938.

The main reason for the purchase was, in fact, nothing to do with codebreaking. The SIS needed a communications centre to pick up the secret signals its network of agents was sending back to Britain from overseas and to radio back their instructions. Bletchley Park was to be a war station with four transmitters and six receivers. During the Munich crisis, the SIS head office staff and those of the GC&CS were put through an evacuation drill. The codebreakers mustered at Bletchley under the thin disguise of 'Captain Ridley's shooting party' – Captain William Ridley being the chief administrative officer of the SIS and thus indirectly responsible for the codebreakers as well as the spies. It's not likely that many of them brought shotguns and it's not game-bird country, but the trial evacuation was a success. GC&CS had tested out the site, a way of sharing the accommodation between the services had been thrashed out, and the codebreakers had found (and discovered the limitations of) the accommodation and attractions of the locality.

Captain W.H.W. Ridley (1887–1955)

William Henry Wake Ridley came from an aristocratic family which included a Viscount and, in later years, one of Margaret Thatcher's rather unloved cabinet ministers. Captain Ridley himself had a naval career: after joining HMS *Britannia* aged 15 he rose steadily through the officer ranks, eventually reaching Captain in 1932. Despite being graded 'zealous and capable' in his various ships during World War I, Ridley never stood out as a naval officer, and the promotion to Captain signalled a sideways move in his career. He would never command a ship – at least not at sea.

Ridley joined the Secret Intelligence Service, and it was under that authority that his 'shooting party' came to Bletchley Park in 1938. During the war, Ridley's role, as MI6's chief administrative officer, was to get things done: in 1941, for example, when every service in the country was swamped with urgent war demands, he ensured that Bletchley got the priority treatment it wanted for building works, transport, labour and so forth. He formally went onto the Royal Navy's retired list in 1947 and was appointed OBE in 1949.

Ridley was one of several senior officers – naval captains, air group captains and brigadiers – in subordinate positions at Bletchley Park, where the inversions of hierarchy required them to report to a mere commander. It may have been no way to run a military operation, but Bletchley Park was different.

Then there was the challenge of recruitment. What was needed was a reserve list, of codebreakers and analysts who could be called up if war was declared. To begin with, there were the old-timers from World War I who might be willing to serve again: Frank Adcock, Frank Birch, Nigel de Grey. And some younger blood would be needed as well, and with the new problem of electro-mechanical cipher devices like Enigma, the new generation should include some with an engineering or mathematical background to work alongside the linguists. Adcock knew where such people could be found: he dined with them regularly at 'high table' in the splendid surroundings of the Hall of King's College, Cambridge. These men (for, in those days, all Fellows of King's were men) could be trusted implicitly, and their intellectual calibre was beyond question. The list of 'available emergency staff' was put together: in its first draft there were nine 'old members', 24 names from Cambridge, 13 from Oxford and various others. Six of the Cambridge names came from King's.

All that remained was to check whether they would agree to serve in this unconventional way. Patrick Wilkinson was a 31-year-old classicist: 'One day in the summer of 1938, after the Nazis had taken over Austria, I was sitting in my rooms at King's when there was a knock on the door. In came F.E. Adcock, accompanied by a small, birdlike man with bright blue eyes whom he introduced as Commander Denniston. He asked whether, in the event of war, I would be willing to do confidential work for the Foreign Office. It sounded interesting, and I said I would. I was thereupon asked to sign the Official Secrets Act form.' Wilkinson went on to explain that the secret was not such a great secret after all. There had been revelations in the late 1920s about the codebreaking achievements of the Admiralty in the previous war, and the King's fellows knew that Adcock had

Nigel de Grey, veteran of Room 40 and later Commander Travis's right-hand man at Bletchley Park.

been part of that group. It didn't take a mathematics professor to put two and two together and work out what the undisclosed confidential work might be.

Some of the Oxbridge dons said no; one of them had died; other names were added to the list and approached. By the end of November, Denniston could report to the Foreign Office that he had been in touch with 'both' universities and that he had a list of about 50 men earmarked for service in the event of war. One, but only one, of the 'men' was a woman, Miss F.M. Ede, a Spanish-language specialist earmarked for work on diplomatic codes. (By March, the emergency list had grown to 73 names, and a second woman, Miss A.M. Dale, had joined Miss Ede on it. Madge Dale [see pages 146–7, Chapter 6] was a classics scholar from Oxford who worked on Italian ciphers, and later, when Italy ceased to be an enemy of Britain, was transferred to work on Japanese codes. Alastair Denniston's efforts to secure equal pay for her, as with other women codebreakers, were unsuccessful.)

In January 1939 there was an induction course. Nine of the recruits – including three from King's College, Cambridge – attended, to learn about transposition ciphers, random number sequences added to code words to hide the code, intelligence and more. As well as Patrick Wilkinson, the King's contingent included one A.M. Turing, who had also received a visit from Adcock and Denniston the previous summer. Turing was earmarked to work on Enigma; Wilkinson Italian Naval traffic.

The men of the Professor type

Adolf Hitler's aggression in the first half of 1939 proved that these measures were not a waste of effort. In March, he tore up the Munich settlement, occupied the rest of Czechoslovakia, and annexed part of Lithuania. Prime Minister Neville Chamberlain issued a 'guarantee' to Poland, committing Britain to a war if Germany were to attack that country. Alastair Denniston mounted a dress-rehearsal for his permanent contingent of codebreakers, sending them off to Bletchley

Park – in due course, known familiarly by its occupants as 'BP' – to try to make the place habitable and more suited to their activities.

When hostilities commenced at the beginning of September, the call-up began. Although it was supposed to be a deadly secret, in these early days there was something amateurish about it all. Patrick Wilkinson described it:

> *The precautions for secrecy were unrealistic, indeed frankly comic. We recruits were not allowed to reveal where we were going, until so many of us had been sighted by acquaintances who were changing trains at Bletchley Junction that the farce was abandoned. A rumour went round the College that one of us, John Saltmarsh, had been made Milk Controller for Glamorgan (if so, why the secrecy?). Another rumour came back to us as we waited: that the obsessively secretive Adcock, on his way up from the station to BP, had been greeted by a small boy with, 'I'll read your secret writing for you, Mister.' In the first few weeks a thriller film came to the Bletchley cinema entitled* The Code of the Secret Service. *It was well attended. As to our work, we were told to say that we were engaged in 'research into the civil air defence of London'.*

Denniston wrote to the Treasury on 3 September 1939, 'For some days now we have been obliged to recruit from our emergency list men of the Professor type who the Treasury agreed to pay at the rate of £600 a year. I attach herewith a list of these gentlemen already called up…'.

Among the men was a small number of actual professors. The list which Denniston had compiled in March named seven professors, one of whom was Adcock. The list also named a certain 'J.R. Tolkien', who was Rawlinson and Bosworth Professor of Anglo-Saxon, contributor to the Oxford English Dictionary, translator of *Beowulf* – and author of *The Hobbit* and, in time, *Lord of The Rings*. But for some reason Tolkien never made it to Bletchley, despite having attended the induction course, for he was told in October 1939 that his services would not be required.

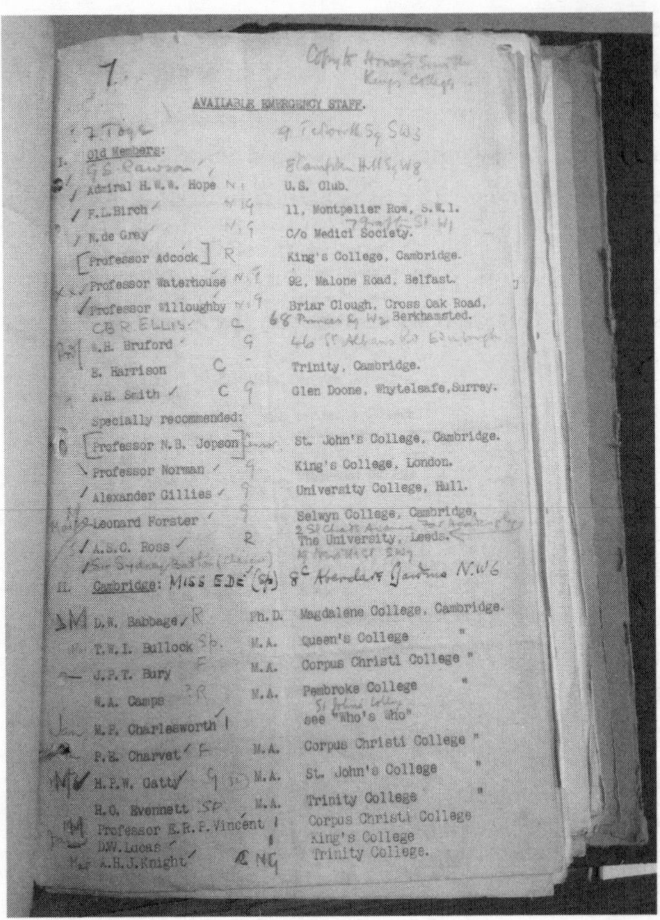

AVAILABLE EMERGENCY STAFF.

I. Old Members:

Admiral H.W.W. Hope	U.S. Club.
F.L.Birch	11, Montpelier Row, S.W.1.
N.de Grey	C/o Medici Society.
Professor Adcock	King's College, Cambridge.
Professor Waterhouse	92, Malone Road, Belfast.
Professor Willoughby	Briar Clough, Cross Oak Road, Berkhamsted.
W.H. Bruford	
E. Harrison	Trinity, Cambridge.
A.H. Smith	Glen Doone, Whyteleafe, Surrey.

Specially recommended:

Professor N.B. Jopson	St. John's College, Cambridge.
Professor Norman	King's College, London.
Alexander Gillies	University College, Hull.
Leonard Forster	Selwyn College, Cambridge.
A.S.C. Ross	The University, Leeds.

II. Cambridge:

D.W. Babbage	Ph.D.	Magdalene College, Cambridge.
T.W.I. Bullock	M.A.	Queen's College "
J.P.T. Bury	M.A.	Corpus Christi College "
W.A. Camps	M.A.	Pembroke College "
M.P. Charlesworth		see "Who's Who"
P.E. Charvet	M.A.	Corpus Christi College "
H.P.W. Gatty	M.A.	St. John's College "
H.O. Evennett	M.A.	Trinity College "
Professor E.R.P. Vincent		Corpus Christi College
D.W. Lucas		King's College
A.H.J. Knight		Trinity College.

A page from the list of 'men of the professor type', potential reservists to be called up to join GC&CS in the event of hostilities.

Several other professors were, however, taken on. Professor Frederick Norman, a linguist from London University, had a vital role in scientific intelligence derived from decrypts. Another professor who was an unlikely choice for Bletchley was Thomas Boase, although he was not on Denniston's original list. He didn't need to be, because Miss Welsford, an 'old member' (to use Denniston's words) of Room 40 was. Rhoda Welsford, like Boase, worked at the Courtauld Institute; Miss Welsford's mother took a lease on the old rectory at Newton Longville, near to Bletchley, where both Professor Boase and Rhoda could be accommodated conveniently as well as in a seemly manner.

Boase had picked up a Military Cross in the previous war, and now he was recruited for the air section, notwithstanding his expertise as an art historian rather than as a codebreaker. (The fact that Boase went off to become Chief Representative at the British Council in the Middle East in 1943 suggests that Commander Travis, by then head of GC&CS, did not find him too indispensable.) Probably it was a good thing that Miss Welsford's connection to Room 40 landed Boase for Bletchley. After the war, her boss at the Courtauld was the Soviet spy Anthony Blunt.

Frederick Norman (1897–1968)

Frederick Norman – nicknamed 'Bimbo', the Italian for a small child, for reasons now forgotten – joined Bletchley Park from King's College, London, where he was Professor of German. He rapidly established a close relationship with Dr R.V. Jones, the young scientist attached to the Intelligence section of the Air Ministry. Norman won Jones' confidence by defusing a rumour: Hitler made a speech on 19 September 1939 which was causing a panic, because apparently he had built a secret weapon against which no counter-measures would be effective. Norman quenched the rumour, by re-translating Hitler's announcement: Hitler had been talking about the Luftwaffe.

Jones described Norman as a 'decidedly excitable professor of German' and was initially scathing about Norman's lack of knowledge of technical matters. But very soon Jones recognized that Norman had a 'nose' which could sniff out what was going on. Jones and Norman had their first joint success against the radio beams which were guiding German bombers to their targets – notably Coventry – during the

Professor Frederick Norman, whose role at Bletchley Park included interpreting coded information about new German technologies including the V-weapons.

Blitz. Decrypts from Bletchley enabled Jones to brief the Air Staff about likely targets and to arrange for decoy radio beams which misdirected the bombers. The Germans kept changing their guidance system, but with Norman's help Jones was able to keep up. A new system referred to in Enigma messages as 'Wotan' was a case in point. Norman explained that Wotan was a one-eyed god in German mythology; Jones interpreted this to mean that the Germans were switching from a two-beam to a single-beam direction-finding and ranging system. Between them, Norman and Jones were able to win the battle of the beams.

Later in the war, Norman was able to unravel the disguised information in coded German messages about the location of radio stations which were vital to the development of the V-weapons. Technical information gleaned from decrypts kept Jones informed about things like the steering mechanism used on V2 rockets, and enabled the Air Staff to bomb the launch sites.

Rhoda Welsford (1894–1975)

As a veteran of Room 40, Rhoda Welsford was on Alastair Denniston's list of likely personnel to be re-recruited for the codebreaking effort needed in a second war against Germany. She is said to have been 'a beautiful blue-stocking', a mixed compliment which probably reflects more on the values of mid-twentieth century commentators than Miss Welsford herself.

She had an upper-class background and a natural aura of command, which those who came across her in her main job as librarian at the Courtauld Institute of Art in London could find strict, even intimidating. The job title obscures the intellect and analytical and organizational abilities she used. Not only did she translate a biography of Tintoretto from Italian into English, but she was the supervisor of the important photographic collection, which kept a record of paintings – of great utility when the originals may be or become inaccessible, stolen or damaged.

At Bletchley Park, she used encoded data sent from a German experimental station at Peenemünde to figure out the flight path and point of impact of pilotless aircraft being tested there. These 'daily trial plots' were superimposed on a different map, with London as the target, helping Air Intelligence get a better understanding of likely launch sites. As to herself, Miss Welsford was described as 'keeping up her Mayfair standards by wearing white gloves as she toiled over the decrypts amid vases of freshly cut flowers.'[2]

From Corpus Christi College, Cambridge, hired over dinner by Adcock, came Professor E.R.P. Vincent, who had written a book in 1927 called *The Italy of the Italians* and went on to edit a translation of Machiavelli's *The Prince.* (Adcock had checked for eavesdroppers behind the door, much to Vincent's amusement, when the secret stuff was discussed.) Vincent was an obvious choice to head up the Italian section, becoming Patrick Wilkinson's boss; later in the war,

2 Cited in Christy Campbell, *Target London.*

once Italy was no longer an enemy, he was promoted to become Assistant Director, taking charge of Cryptographic Coordination and Records, the purpose of which was to ensure streamlining and efficiency across the whole Bletchley Park organization. This was no easy task given that the need-to-know principle kept different groups isolated. Vincent was also chairman of the social committee in the early years of the war: musical and theatrical as well as dances. ('Vincent was a very keen dancer, sampling a succession of young partners but always chaperoned by his delightfully good-natured wife.')[3] He finished the war with a CBE in recognition of his contribution.

One old-timer who could not get on with Vincent was the acerbic W.F. Clarke, who noted that 'the first big row' began over the use of his long-standing assistant Miss White. It was a case of gendered role-descriptions getting in the way of substance. Theoretically, Miss White was a secretary; technically, Clarke had been using her as a cryptanalyst, and with her years of experience she was a poor fit with the professorial newcomers, who were 'jealous of her, realizing she was better at the job than they; in fact she often had to teach them their job and point out their mistakes'. It appears that Miss White didn't help matters much, and she was transferred; Clarke's legacy was a sort of threat ('the full correspondence on this matter will be found in my files labelled The White Conspiracy').

Connections, conspiracy and crosswords

Bletchley Park's expansion, once the war got going in earnest following the fall of France in 1940, meant that recruits had to come from circles outside academia. Much has been made of the crossword competition run by the *Daily Telegraph* in January 1942, the challenge being to solve the puzzle in 12 minutes in exam conditions. The contest was invigilated by Colonel Freddie Nichols of MI8, who invited the

3 Patrick Wilkinson, *Facets of a Life, 1986.*

successful candidates to see him 'on a matter of national importance'. But in fact very few people were recruited in this way. Word-of-mouth and family connections were far more significant.

Peter Calvocoressi, a barrister in peacetime, volunteered for the army in 1940. At the War Office he was subjected to various tests to determine his suitability; at the end of the day 'I arrived in an office where the accumulated results of the day's experiences lay tabulated on a sheet of paper with, at the foot, a verdict. Although from where I sat it was upside down, I could read it clearly enough. It ran: "No good, even for intelligence."' Nonetheless, a work colleague put him in contact with the Director of Intelligence in the Air Ministry, which led to Calvocoressi joining Bletchley Park. 'In some ways I was a fairly typical member of BP. Besides possessing certain basic qualifications such as knowledge of German I came from the right educational establishments and I belonged more rather than less to a world where people looking for recruits would look – a restricted middle-class professional world where it was comparatively easy to get trustworthy reports about individuals.'

Word of mouth, or the old-boy network as some people call it, is simply a form of social networking. The Oxbridge network led the professors to Bletchley, and indeed some of the professor types were not, in fact, men at all. Although Denniston's pre-war recruitment list reflected the makeup of professor-level posts at British universities in the 1930s – that is to say, with hardly a woman in sight – academic women joined Bletchley Park in abundance. Several went on to become professors in their later careers, when the glass ceiling was less formal and occasionally had loft hatches. Bletchley was, reluctantly, coming to terms with the war for talent. ('I could not face the prospect of having our vacancies filled 100 per cent by women' and, as regards 11 vacancies for linguists, 'of these five must be men. The remainder could be women, if these were really first-class people' are among several toe-curling remarks to be found in the National Archives.) In 1942, when those linguist vacancies were being filled, at least one recruit came from the then-all-female Girton College, Cambridge. This was Alison Fairlie, who was elected to a professorship in later years. It seems rather likely that these first-class women were a contrast to the five male recruits, who presumably included some who were only second-class.

Having Oliver Strachey, who had been immersed for years in the fight for women's rights, in a senior position meant that his wife Ray could get first-class recruits from the all-female Newnham College, Cambridge. Another recruitment agent, the female Oxford counterpart to Frank Adcock, was Lynda Grier, who since 1921 had been the Principal of Lady Margaret Hall (LMH). Miss Grier had known Alastair Denniston's wife Dorothy from the days before the previous war, when Dorothy was a student at LMH, and the connection to a source of talent was made. So, among a large cohort of graduates from LMH came the academics Dione Clementi, Anne Glyn-Jones, and Madge Dale herself, who was also destined to become a professor.

Dione Clementi (1914–2010)

'Security was never more secure than with her,' commented Jocelyn Kerslake, who had known Dione Clementi from the time they were undergraduates together at Lady Margaret Hall, Oxford, and who found themselves thrown together in Hut 4 at Bletchley Park in 1941. Jocelyn wanted to know what her friend had been detailed to work on – but even though they were in the same Hut, this was an Official Secret, and Dione would not say. In fact, it had to do with analysis of captured German documents, on which Hut 4 depended for breaking Naval Enigma.

Dione Clementi was a history graduate whose career was in academia: at the Universities of London and Manchester, with periods in between at the British School in Rome and back at LMH in Oxford. Her father had been Governor of Hong Kong as well as a scholar and linguist in his own right, who, perhaps unusually among his generation, was enthusiastic about his daughter's wish to pursue an academic career 'rather than a social one'.[4] Her specialism was medieval history, publishing works on the Norman Kingdom of Sicily, the Holy Roman Emperor Henry VI, and more. She (like Alan Turing) was never a full professor, but (again like him) was a Reader, which is the next best thing.

Churchill's liver

The newly-arrived codebreakers, whether middle-class professionals, professors or otherwise, had to live somewhere. Not everyone was as fortunate as Professor Boase in knowing someone with a spare room in a rectory. In January 1939, people had been asked to register officially any spare rooms – any at all. The result was that billeting officers allocated the arrivals to families around the town of Bletchley and the surrounding villages. The experiences were not uniformly welcoming, and in some cases downright unpleasant. Sometimes the accommodation was a surprise: an 'unfurnished boxroom'; 'loo at the bottom of the garden'; 'no gas or electricity'. Sometimes it was the food: '[the landlady's] idea of a good main meal was a tin of pink salmon heated through with mashed potato'; 'breakfast was left-overs from the evening meal, kept for four hours in the oven'. What was also unpredictable was the character of the householders on whom the characters from Bletchley Park were imposed. Sometimes

4 Obituary by Jocelyn Kerslake, *Lady Margaret Hall Annual Record.*

the hosts were superlatively good, with long-lasting relationships formed with the local family; for others, things went less well, with codebreakers recalling lights being switched off at the mains to save electricity (not much fun for shift-workers whose 'day' was in the hours of darkness), or witnesses to domestic tensions.

For Patrick Wilkinson, one of the first to arrive, things were at the better end of the spectrum. He found himself billeted on the pub landlord at Great Brickhill, a few miles south of Bletchley:

> *The landlord was Frank Stabb, a Devonian ex-policeman, rubicund, round-bellied, 'no nonsense' but warm-hearted – the image of 'mine host'.... Mrs Stabb was an excellent plain cook, though the materials on which she could exercise her art diminished sadly in quantity and quality as the War went on. The Stabbs did all they could to keep up culinary standards. Thus Frank reared, on the scraps from the table, two very large pigs called Roosevelt and Churchill. Some parts of them the Food Controller allowed him to retain; and one Christmas morning we breakfasted on Churchill's liver.*

Alongside Wilkinson at the Duncombe Arms was Gordon Welchman, also from Cambridge; despite being a newcomer and, as a mathematician, something of an outsider among the linguists, he brought ideas about how the Bletchley Park organization ought to be run effectively, which may not have endeared him to the veterans who knew the answer from the previous 'show'. Mathematicians were still a novelty, as the specialisms of the 'men of the Professor type' suggest.

From King's College there were, over the course of the war, no fewer than 13 fellows of King's and eight non-fellow members of King's at Bletchley Park. This is certainly disproportionate, and what is perhaps surprising is that many of the Kingsmen actually fitted in and made a substantial impact. Surprising, because in the 1920s and early 1930s, King's College was not noted for selecting its fellows for their intellectual greatness or Nobel prize-winning potential. Of course, there were exceptions, like John Maynard Keynes and Dilly Knox; and King's had its share of famous alumni like the poets Rupert Brooke and Xu Zhimo. Some fellows, like Sir Frank Adcock, F.L. Lucas and Alan Turing (see pages 95–7, Chapter 4) had distinguished academic careers – as well as distinguished roles in secret intelligence – but in general, it was more important to King's that a fellowship candidate would fit in well in the collegiate society which characterized the college in the interwar period. Apart from some rare mathematicians, the academic backgrounds of the Kingsmen at Bletchley was predominantly in the arts and humanities: classics, languages, history.

The King's High Table

According to the official history of MI5, one-third of the King's 'High Table' – the fellows of the college – were at Bletchley Park in World War II. Here is a selection of these men and their roles.

	Academic career	**Work and life at Bletchley**
Philip Hall (1904–82) (fellow 1927–82)	Mathematician, FRS, President of the London Mathematical Society, Sadleirian Professor of Pure Mathematics	Italian Naval, then Japanese Naval.

D.W. Lucas (1905–85) (fellow 1929–85)	Classicist	Italian Naval, then Japanese Naval. Brother of F.L. Lucas, but disliked his time at BP.
Christopher Morris (1906–93) (fellow 1930–93)	Historian	German Naval hand-ciphers. Described his work as 'Bletchley's poor relations' (in contrast to the glitzy Enigma).
J.H. Plumb (1911–2001) (fellow 1939–46)	Historian, Master of Christ's College, Cambridge, Professor of History, knighted in 1982	German, Italian and later Japanese Naval, and traffic analysis.
John Saltmarsh (1908–74) (fellow 1931–74)	Historian	The cartographic expert of Hut 3: German Army and Air Force map reconstruction from coded references.
Alexis Vlasto (1915–2000) (fellow 1945–50)	Linguist, eventually specializing in Russian	Japanese Air Force codes. Became Wing-Commander in the RAF 'but I never actually flew'. Married another BP codebreaker.
Patrick Wilkinson (1907–85) (fellow 1932–85)	Classicist	Italian Naval, then Hut 3 intelligence. Married another BP codebreaker.

F.L. ('Peter') Lucas (1894–1967)

F.L. ('Peter') Lucas started his career in the traditional way, as a classicist. World War I interrupted, in which he suffered five wounds at the Somme but survived to take a role in the Intelligence Corps. After the war he was elected by King's College, Cambridge, to a fellowship in classics, but he became one of the first lecturers in English when Cambridge eventually decided that it was a proper subject for a degree.

King's College, Cambridge, in the 1920s was closely associated with the Bloomsbury Group, with the economist John Maynard Keynes its best-known member. Lucas was connected as well, becoming involved in a number of triangular relationships involving Bloomsbury people of both sexes, typical of the Group's bohemian way of life.

Lucas' career in the study of English literature developed in the interwar period. He was an opponent of the new school of literary criticism led by F.R. Leavis. While Lucas preferred Elizabethan drama and wanted his students to consider context, dates and the writers' character, the modern approach was to treat text on its own terms. Lucas' assessment of more modern writers was hardly positive: 'How is one to mark in an examination the assertion that Gerard Manley Hopkins was the greatest poet of his century? One may think the author of such a remark almost certifiable.'

As World War II loomed, he became known as an opponent of fascism and appeasement; it is said that Goebbels put Lucas on his extermination list. At Bletchley Park, Lucas was allocated to Hut 3 and helped organize it for intelligence analysis and research. He also commanded the Bletchley Park detachment of the Home Guard. In 1940 their job was deadly serious, with the threat of German invasion an immediate one. Lucas arranged for the digging of trenches and establishment of defence positions to give the codebreakers enough time to destroy their secret papers if the Germans got as far as Bletchley. At the war's end, Lucas was awarded the OBE for his contribution at Bletchley Park, and then he returned to King's, to writing, teaching and the study of literature from other countries.

Whatever you might make of the recruitment methods of the Government Code & Cypher School, it had undoubtedly worked well in choosing two fellows of King's College, Cambridge. These two were to make the crucial difference in solving the one problem which the senior staff, notably Alastair Denniston, knew to be unsolvable. That problem was the Enigma machine, and the Kingsmen concerned were Alfred Dillwyn Knox and Alan Mathison Turing. By the time war broke out, both men had been studying the problem for some time. And Knox, who had been working on it for longer, had already figured out a way of breaking Enigma.

CHAPTER 3

Illicit Services Knox

Arthur Scherbius' invention gave birth to the most famous codebreaking challenge of World War II, and to the most impressive achievements of Dilly Knox. Scherbius' idea was that electric wiring could be used to substitute each letter from a message, and that by placing the wires into rotors the substitutions could themselves change each time the rotors were moved.

Scherbius' machine was a big thing. It was shaped like a typewriter with some inelegant knobs sticking out of the side. The typist would type in the text, but because it was a cipher machine the actual type appearing on the paper was transformed into nonsense. The rotors which changed the encipherment were moved using the knobs at the side. The machine was not a success. It was much too heavy and unreliable. Scherbius tried again, this time replacing the typing mechanism with torch bulbs, which lit up one at a time under a panel which showed the letters of the alphabet in little circular windows. This was the 'glowlamp machine', according to Scherbius' marketing material, and its brand name was 'Enigma'. This trimmed-down machine was demonstrated at the International Postal Congress in 1924, where it immediately attracted interest from not only potential commercial buyers but also diplomats and military personnel from several countries. This new Enigma exceeded all expectations: eventually, according to some estimates, 100,000 Enigma machines were made.

Unfortunately for Arthur Scherbius, all this lay in the future. The period of development of the machines coincided with the postwar hyperinflation in Germany, during which many people lost all they had. Scherbius struggled to keep afloat, and it took until 1928 for his company, Chiffriermaschinen AG, to stabilize. It had undertaken a capital-raising exercise, and old losses were still being paid off; the company never paid any dividends although it managed to stay solvent. The final tragedy was the death of Scherbius in a road accident in 1929 – years before Germany scaled up her armed forces, and the number of Enigma machines with it.

Still, the German armed forces began experimenting with the machine in the period 1926–28, and radio-towers in Poland began to pick up signals enciphered with the new device. Unlike coded messages, where words and phrases were replaced by groups of numbers (as in the codes used for the Zimmermann Telegram), the Enigma machine was a substitution cipher, changing each letter one by one into something else. Old-fashioned ciphers were easy to break, because some letters occur more frequently than others in regular language, so counting letters could often reveal the substitution pattern; but because the Wehrmacht Enigma changed the encipherment every time the rotors

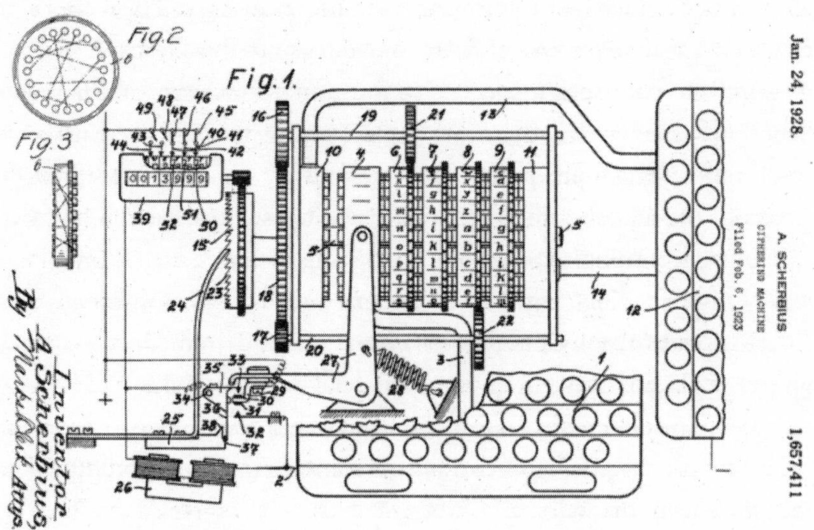

A diagram from Arthur Scherbius' 1928 patent application for his Enigma machine.

moved – in fact, every time a new letter was typed into the machine – the frequency-counting attack didn't work. A completely new approach would be needed.

The Wehrmacht Enigma

The Enigma machine used by the German Army and Air Force used a typewriter-like configuration for both encipherment and decipherment: so long as both sender and receiver had set up their machines the same way, the same setting would work to encrypt and to decrypt the message. The set-up was all-important, because each variable component played an important role in transforming (enciphering) the secret message.

The Wehrmacht machine had four variable features, each of which could change the encipherment:

- The selection of rotors. At the start of the war, there were five rotors (which the codebreakers called 'wheels') to choose from. The machine could take three: the choice of which three and in which order gave no fewer than 60 possibilities before any of the other variable features had been settled. (Later, the German Navy introduced additional rotors and different versions of the 'reflector' disc which turned the electric current back for a second pass through the rotors.)
- The ring-setting of each rotor. Each rotor has wiring inside it which transforms each letter of the alphabet into something else (or, in some cases, leaves it unaltered). But the wiring is housed in a 'core' surrounded by a moveable ring (called the 'tyre' by the codebreakers).

The ring-setting determined at which point the next rotor would move on, as well as confusing the question of how the core wiring of the rotor was orientated at the start of encryption. With 26 different settings on each rotor, and three rotors in the machine, there were potentially 26 × 26 × 26 = 17,576 options for ring-settings.

- The orientation of each rotor. To set up their machines the same way, the sending and receiving operator needed to know which letter on each rotor's ring was uppermost, and so visible through the machine's lid, at the start of the encipherment process. Again, there are 26 possible orientations for each rotor, so another 17,576 possibilities. Just to make life difficult for eavesdroppers, a new starting position was chosen for every single message.
- The plugboard. At the front of the Enigma machine is a set of sockets, two (in and out) for each letter of the alphabet. This also interchanged the letters in the text being enciphered. During World War II German practice was to use ten cables, so switching 20 letters into something else while leaving six unaltered. There are 150 million-million options for ten cross-pluggings.

First, though, the codebreakers needed to get access to the hardware. In the 1920s, when Scherbius was marketing his device to any and all comers, the British had bought an Enigma machine. On analysis, they decided it was actually quite easy to break. Provided you could guess at some part of the content of the message, you could exploit the characteristic of the machine that no letter could encipher as itself. This enabled the codebreaker to eliminate large numbers of possible arrangements of the three rotors in the machine, and eventually find out how the rotors were configured at the beginning of encipherment. Once they had this information, it was all plain sailing. The result was that Enigma was deemed to be too insecure for British Service use, and the Enigma was filed and forgotten.

Rodding

That began to change in 1936. Civil war had broken out in Spain, and the dictators of Europe were rallying round to support General Franco and his Nationalists. The Germans provided Enigma machines to the Spanish Nationalists and to Mussolini's Italians, who were able to communicate with each other in apparent security. Their Morse Code messages were picked up in France and copies were given to GC&CS, because the British were concerned about the consequences the war might have for the security of Gibraltar. At GC&CS they found their way to the desk of Dilly Knox. 'In 1936, for the first time, Dilly began to refuse his invitations to the [King's College] Founder's Feast. The reason was simple; the dinner was noted, even among Cambridge colleges, for its hospitality and its fine wines, and, in consequence, for the occasional indiscretions of the guests. These, to be sure, were heard by Kingsmen only, but the time had come when Dilly could not risk even the hint of a shadow of a reference to what he was doing.'[5]

Dilly Knox (1884–1943)

Dilly Knox is such a dominant figure in the story of Bletchley Park that any record about codebreaking there is in danger of becoming an extended biography of him.

5 Penelope Fitzgerald, *The Knox Brothers* (1977), p. 194.

The German armed forces' version of the Enigma machine, showing the plugboard at the front, the keyboard, the panel of lamps, and (at the rear) the tops of the three coding rotors.

To begin with, his family. Dilly was the second of four sons of the Anglican Bishop of Manchester. Each of these four was a hyper-achiever: Edmund, the eldest, became editor of the satirical magazine *Punch*, known by his pen-name Evoe; the two younger ones were men of the church. Ronald, the youngest, converted with a blaze of publicity to the Catholic faith, becoming a Monsignor, and translator of the Bible for the British Catholic population. The other, Wilfred 'was an Anglo-Catholic priest in the East End, a dedicated socialist, a fearless motor-bike rider, a welfare worker, an eccentric recluse and just possibly a saint.'[6] There were also two sisters, Ethel and Winnie, but they never stood a chance to shine with these four as brothers.

Dilly himself was known to be a little cantankerous and more than a little eccentric. The cantankerousness was exceptional rather than typical, though there were certainly times when he spoke his mind. The eccentricity was undeniable. The stories abound: spectacles kept in his tobacco pouch, the terrifying experience of being driven by Dilly at high speed in the countryside, forgetting to invite his brothers to his wedding – some of them may even be true. What perhaps does not come out so often is that Dilly had 'an oddly romantic side to his nature, a natural grace and shy gallantry.' He was a great dancer and had great loyalty to his subordinates and younger members of his family. His niece, the future novelist Penelope Fitzgerald, was brought back to school late by Dilly to face the wrath of the housemistress. 'Rules are made to be kept,' she said. Dilly's response was: 'But they are defined only by being broken.'

---

6 Richard Holmes, 'Introduction' in Penelope Fitzgerald, *The Knox Brothers* (1977).

Dilly was uncomfortable with the changes that World War II brought to his academic world of cryptanalysis. As Bletchley Park turned into a species of industrial complex there were changes at the top which distressed him: the old management, in the person of Alastair Denniston, had known better how to handle Dilly and to get the best out of him. The usual pattern was that Dilly would resign: 'My dear Denniston … These statistics [punched cardboard codebreaking sheets] must be handed over at once … My personal feelings on the matter are so strong that unless they leave by Wednesday night I shall tender my resignation' (January 1940); 'My dear Denniston … To concede your monstrous theory of collecting material for others is impossible for a scholar … rendering it impossible for me to work at Bletchley Park' (November 1941). Denniston's strength was to handle Dilly's blackmail attempts with firmness and care. 'My dear Dilly … I am glad that you are frank and open with me … If you do design a super Rolls-Royce that is no reason why you should yourself drive the thing … more especially if you are not a very good driver… You are Knox, a scholar with a European reputation, who knows more about the inside of a machine than anyone else. The exigencies of war need that latter gift of yours though few people are aware of it … I do disagree with you. Yours ever, A.G.D.' The bite in this was hardly hidden: Knox had nearly crippled himself in a car accident.

Denniston also knew Dilly well enough to realize that things were not right with him. Dilly's letter of November 1941 begins with the understatement 'I am in the doctor's hands for a minor ailment.' It was the early stage of something much more serious. It was cancer, which took Dilly from the world in February 1943 aged only 58. Mavis Lever visited him in hospital where 'his brother Evoe was by his bedside and they were roaring with laughter composing Dilly's last words.'

Dilly Knox, GC&CS' Chief Cryptographer, and leader of the British attack on Enigma.

The Enigma machine on which the Italians were communicating with the Spanish was slightly different from the one purchased by MI6 in the 1920s. The 'stepping mechanism', by which the middle and left-hand rotors were moved on after the right-hand one had gone through a complete cycle, was different, and the internal wiring in the rotors was different from the commercially-available machine. Dilly Knox was not fazed by these differences. He reckoned that Italians would like as not begin their messages with the Italian for 'to': this was how the Italian Navy had addressed coded messages amongst themselves. If that were so, the letters P, E, and R should not ever be found as the first three letters of the message, because an Enigma machine could never encipher a letter as itself. This tiny crack in the Enigma's security was enough for Knox to force the Italian version of the machine wide open.

Knox then developed a system of 'rods' to find the way the Enigma users had set up their machines. The principle behind the rods was that the substitution done by the middle and left rotors of the machine did not change, provided that the stepping mechanism had not activated.

For stretches of 26 consecutive letters of a message, the only changing part of the Enigma was the rotation of the right-hand rotor. This enabled Knox to work out, for each possible combination of left and middle rotors, the transformative effect of those 'static' rotors. These effects were written onto little cardboard rods, which could then be tried out systematically to identify the rotors in use and their start positions. And then decipherment of the messages could happen.

When war broke out in 1939 between Britain and Germany, the successes which Knox had had with the Enigma machine in the Spanish Civil War were of limited use. The problem was that the German armed forces were using a version of Enigma which had sophisticated modifications and different internal wiring – against which the rods technique was useless. But when, at the end of the German *blitzkrieg* against France, Italy came into the war, the utility of rodding was reborn.

The Enigma family (1923–41)

There is more than one type of Enigma machine. Different versions have appeared at different times in the Enigma story, for different purposes. Here is a selection:

1923 Scherbius' original model with a typed printout. The printing mechanism was its Achilles heel, and he quickly replaced it with the 'commercial model' which could not print.

1924 The first of a new type of machine – Enigma A, with light-bulbs to show the enciphered output – was exhibited at the International Postal Congress in Stockholm. It had the now-familiar keyboard, lamps and three rotors, and its rotors moved on mechanically every time a key was pressed. Some of these machines had extra keys for letters with accents: Å, Ä and Ö.

1927 The Enigma K, which appeared to have a fourth rotor, became available. This was the principal commercial Enigma variant. The fourth rotor was, in fact, a 'reflector' which could be turned by hand to create additional settings.

1929 The German armed forces' interest in Enigma led to the addition of the plugboard as an extra security device. The basic model was the Enigma I (army and air force), adapted for the navy as the Enigma M1.

1931 The German military intelligence service (Abwehr) introduced a new machine – Enigma G – without a plugboard but with four rotors, each of which had several 'turnover notches' forcing the adjacent rotor to move on one step. This machine also had a settable reflector and a special crank to drive the stepping mechanism.

1941 For the U-boat arm of the German Navy, a different four-rotor machine was brought into service – Enigma M4. This retained the plugboard, and the fourth rotor was a special thin one which could only be used in the left-most position and did not rotate during encipherment.

When Cunningham won at Matapan

At the start of the war, Knox had set up shop in the cottages in the stable yard next to the main mansion building at Bletchley Park. Here he had a 'research section' which was working on the most intractable codebreaking problems, and the most remarkable feature of Knox's section was that his staff consisted almost entirely of young women. One of them, Mavis Lever, explained that it was not because Dilly was a womanizer; his recruits were selected by the formidable Miss Moore of the Foreign Office, who interviewed everyone first. 'Dilly had made it clear that he did not want any debutantes whose daddies had got them into Bletchley through knowing someone'; his girls were all qualified as linguists or students of literature. He needed people who could find patterns and fit them together, just as he himself had done with the Mimes of Herodas at the time of the previous war.

Mavis Lever described her first arrival at Bletchley Park, where Knox had about eight other women working alongside him. 'Taking his pipe out of his mouth, he looked up and said: "We're breaking machines. Have you got a pencil?"... He then handed me a bunch of gobbledegook messages made worse by his purple inky scrawls over them and said: "Here, have a go." ... "But I am afraid it's all Greek to me," I said in despair, at which he burst into delighted laughter and said: "I wish it were." I felt very embarrassed when I discovered that he was a distinguished Greek scholar.'

Mavis Lever would become one of the most trusted achievers in Knox's team. One day, she just happened to notice that an intercepted message did not contain the letter 'L'. Even being able to see that, in a message of random gobbledegook, was impressive; she instantly recognized that the message was a practice message, with dummy content. The bored Enigma operator, ordered to send something meaningless, had just kept pressing the 'L' key on his machine, so the enciphered message had no Ls in it. Mavis now had a perfect 'crib' – guessed-at plain-text – from which she, and a young man from Hut 6 called Keith Batey, could derive the Enigma settings being used.

Mavis Lever (1921–2013)

Mavis Lever came to codebreaking from University College, London. She said it all started because Joseph Goebbels, the German propaganda minister, was promoting tourist holidays in 1936, when Mavis was a teenager. Joining 'crowds of happy German workers with free tickets ... to be indoctrinated into the myths and legends of German heroes' in a steamer trip along the Rhine, Mavis had a fine time and decided to study German literature. When war broke out, the college was evacuated to Aberystwyth, where 'I wanted to do something better for the war effort than read poetry in Wales, so I said I'd train as a nurse, but I was told: "Oh, no you don't. Not with your German."' So, Mavis found herself being interviewed by Miss Moore at the Foreign Office and sent to Broadway Buildings, near St James' Park in London, working on commercial codes. Her sharpness was spotted early on when she uncovered an illegal shipment to Germany, and she was quickly transferred to Dilly Knox's Cottage group at Bletchley Park.

After the war, Mavis stayed on at GC&CS, now rebranded as GCHQ, working on Russian codes until 1947. She travelled to Canada with her husband Keith who had taken a role at the High Commission, and they started a family. Back in Britain in the 1960s, Mavis began a new career as a garden historian, writing books and campaigning for the protection of historic gardens and landscapes against the bulldozers driving motorways across the countryside. She received an MBE for this work, though nothing for her contribution to Dilly Knox's team at Bletchley Park.

The women had different roles: Claire Harding acted in some way as office manager, which was probably necessary given Dilly's somewhat chaotic style. She organized the shift pattern and work allocation, ensured that the rods were put away into the correct jam jar alongside other rods from the same set, and even made arrangements along with

Mavis Lever, whose codebreaking achievements included breaking messages revealing the whereabouts of the Italian fleet, facilitating victory at the Battle of Matapan.

Elizabeth Grainger for Alan Turing to have coffee and sandwiches sent up to his hideout in the stable loft. The 'girls' included Mrs Balance, the mother of one of the codebreaking team, who had been brought in as tea lady to avoid the accidents which might happen with people like Dilly 'wrestling with a cantankerous urn'.

The team, and Mavis Lever – who in due time would become Mavis Batey – achieved their great triumph in March 1941. By this point in the war, Italy had come in on the German side, and a battle for dominance in North Africa was in full progress. Britain needed to protect the Suez Canal, while Italy aimed for control of the whole south-eastern Mediterranean. Admiral Cunningham, based at Alexandria, was determined to prevent the supply of Italy's army, dependent on seaborne supply from the home country, and at the same time to ensure the safety of convoys trying to support and resupply the British in Egypt and the Middle East. The Eastern Mediterranean was the vital naval theatre, and the Italian Navy was the primary enemy.

The Italian armed forces were still using the relatively unsophisticated version of Enigma which was vulnerable to attack by Knox's methods. Fortunately for Cunningham, Italian signals staff used a word rather copiously. This word was XALTX, which was Italian telegraphese for 'stop'. Bizarrely, they ended each message with a stop, and used the dummy letter X to fill up the code-groups so there was always a multiple of five letters for the whole message. That meant that a message might end with the sequence 'XALTXXXX' – providing the codebreakers with an excellent crib. Under Dilly Knox's leadership the girls produced charts enabling them to derive rotor information from XALTX sequences.

'On 25 March,' said Mavis Lever, 'we broke a signal which said, quite simply, with the minimum of topping and tailing, "Today is X minus 3," but even in such a short message the operator had inserted three full stops. Our XALTX charts were put to good use and, as Dilly quipped, success added a new meaning to the word exaltation.' The message was relayed to Cunningham in Alexandria.

Cunningham was fully aware that his every move was being shadowed by the Japanese consul, so he did not immediately set sail. He went to play golf, and made sure the consul overheard him discussing plans for dinner later that evening. As darkness fell, Cunningham slipped back aboard, and the fleet sailed at 7 pm. It was all very well to know that the Italian fleet was going to conduct a major operation on 28 March, but it would be too coincidental by half if the British Mediterranean Fleet should just show up in the perfect place at just the wrong time. So, a light reconnaissance aircraft was sent up to 'spot' the Italians – the observations of which provided an ideal cover story for the successful interception, and the devastation of the Italian Fleet which followed. It was called the Battle of Cape Matapan and it was the first unqualified naval success of the war. It was also the end of Italian naval dominance in the Mediterranean.

There were celebrations at Bletchley, even though the aeroplane was taking all the credit. The success was all over the news and the girls were dying to tell their families about it. Of course, that was wholly forbidden, but Cunningham knew what had helped him to victory and visited Bletchley Park to thank the team in person. (The girls played a terrible practical joke on the Admiral, encouraging him to lean against a recently whitewashed wall in his immaculate navy blue home-waters uniform. His reaction is not recorded.) For his part, Knox composed some verse, crediting every member of his group of girls, while delivering some sideswipes at the now-famous spotter plane. Some of the rhymes are worthy of the poet Herodas, no less:

For Claire Harding there was this:

When Cunningham won at Matapan
By the grace of God and Claire,
For she pilots well the aeroplane
That spotted their fleet from the air.

For Phyllida Cross, one of his girls, the rhyme was particularly awful:

When Cunningham won at Matapan
By the grace of God and Phyllida,
And made that impossibly self-willed girl
If possible self-willeder.

For Mavis herself, a classical allusion:

When Cunningham won at Matapan
By the grace of God and Mavis,
Nigro simillima cygno est, *praise Heaven,*
A very rara avis.[7]

7 *Nigro simillima cygno est*: it is very like a black swan; *rara avis*: an exotic bird

There was even an honourable mention for the tea lady:

When Cunningham won at Matapan
By the grace of God and Mrs Balance,
Indeed, he said, the Cottage team
Is a team of all the talents.

It did not quite end there. The normally acerbic W.F. Clarke, who was by this time head of the Italian naval section in Hut 4, added a verse of his own, giving credit where it was properly due:

When Cunningham won at Matapan
By the grace of God and Dilly,
He was the brains behind them all
And should ne'er be forgotten. Will he?

A lever and a rock

Whatever the rationale behind his recruitment method, Dilly's staff (sometimes described, with political incorrectness, as 'Dilly's fillies') included some exceptional talent. One of the most exceptional was Margaret Rock, who was a mathematician rather than a linguist. She joined the team of girls in April 1940, but made her mark on a new species of Enigma problem which came to light some time after the successes against the Italian Navy.

Margaret Rock (1903–83)

At 37, Margaret Rock should never have been classified as one of Dilly's 'girls' when she joined the Research section in the Bletchley Park Cottages in April 1940. She was already a respected statistician working for what is now the Confederation of British Industry, a role she had had since leaving university.

Margaret was fortunate to be placed in a school in Portsmouth which pushed its girls to achieve in areas not traditional for young women in the early twentieth century. So, when Margaret developed a talent for mathematics, she was able to go on to Bedford College, London, to study for a degree in Mathematics and French. This led to her postgraduation work on statistics.

Bletchley Park provided a new direction to her career. Her first triumph was working with Dilly Knox on the Abwehr version of the Enigma; she was also deployed on some secret projects unknown to the rest of the Research section. At the end of the war she was given the MBE and kept on at GCHQ, eventually reaching the retirement age of 65 there. By this time, she was living with her lifelong friend Norah Sheward (who has been described as a 'domineering and bossy woman, a contrast to the quiet self-assurance of Margaret'). Ten years into retirement, the Bletchley story began to trickle out, but Margaret contributed little, the importance of silence influenced by her much more recent GCHQ work. However, she continued her friendship with Mavis Lever (by now Mavis Batey) until Margaret's death.

Indeed, when Italy dropped out of the Axis in 1943, the Italian naval intelligence work at Bletchley came to an end: Professor Vincent, and his team including Patrick Wilkinson from King's College, Cambridge, were redeployed, mostly onto Japanese codes. For Knox's group, however, the work had not dried up. For in mid-1941, the volume of material from one of the 'outlying Enigmas' had risen to a level where Knox's research section could get its teeth into it properly.

This traffic had first been observed in late 1939. Although plainly enciphered on an Enigma-like device, it was different from the standard military Enigma. Knox's team got to work and derived the structure of the machine being used. It had four rotors – or rather, the 'reflector' device which in a military Enigma was fixed, was 'settable' into different positions for different messages – and many more turnover notches per rotor. It had no plugboard, which made things simpler for the codebreakers. Soon they were able to unravel the secret information telling message recipients how to orientate their rotors for decryption, and the new type of Enigma traffic began to reveal itself. The secret was that the multiple turnover notches sometimes led all four rotors to step on together. Knox, in characteristic Alice-in-Wonderland style, named these phenomena 'crabs' and 'lobsters'. 'The hunt was up and the scent was good,' wrote Knox to Denniston. 'One very fine Lobster among others was caught and after two days Miss Lever, by very good and careful work, succeeded in an evaluation ... to ascertain the green wheel.' Once the wiring of the rotors had been ascertained, the process of decryption could begin.

It soon transpired that these unusual Enigma machines were being used by the Abwehr. The Enigma messages tended to be directions to local Abwehr outstations instructing them on the intelligence the Germans needed, and the reports back. The valuable insights these gave into German knowledge, and its limits, founded a new species of British special intelligence, called ISK, which stood for Intelligence Services Knox. Actually, the insiders at Bletchley Park re-named the acronym Illicit Services Knox, since the Abwehr was often operating where it should not be. ISK was the ultimate triumph of Dilly Knox, though he did not live to see the value which it contributed to the war effort.

Abwehr agents used hand ciphers, rather than the Enigma machine; these were also broken with great success by a team at Bletchley under Oliver Strachey (see pages 40–41, Chapter 1). Because the nature of the cryptanalysis was different from that needed for machine ciphers, his section was separate from ISK, and named ISOS, for Intelligence (or Illicit) Services Oliver Strachey. Again, the value of the material coming out of ISOS was priceless.

ISK, in particular, provided details on what the Germans were watching in the Straits of Gibraltar in 1942, when the Alamein battles were taking place and the build-up to the invasion of North Africa by American and British troops (Operation Torch) was going on. The use of ISK intelligence continued as the Germans were driven out of North Africa and the Allies planned to invade Sicily, an intention which had as much as possible to be disguised. By monitoring the Abwehr, ISK was able to show that the deception plans – including the famous 'Man Who Never Was', a corpse dressed to look like an intelligence officer carrying (fake) plans, deliberately allowed to be washed up on the Spanish coast – had successfully duped the Germans.

ISK and ISOS also allowed the British to monitor the success of deception plans much later in the war, in particular just before the Normandy landings. It was vital to encourage the Germans to believe that the main thrust of the invasion of Northern Europe would come via the Dover straits, so as to lead them to keep a significant force in that area, and thereby relieve pressure from the invaders in Normandy. Once again complex arrangements to disguise the Allied intentions were put in place, reported on to the Abwehr by 'German spies' in Britain who were in fact working for British Intelligence. The Abwehr signals, open to Bletchley Park, showed that these deceptions were also succeeding.

By this time, Alfred Dillwyn Knox had succumbed to the cancer which had begun its course in 1941. However, it was under his leadership that Mavis Lever, together with her husband-to-be Keith Batey, as well as Margaret Rock, had cracked the problem of the Abwehr Enigma. As Knox said, 'Give me a Rock and a Lever and I can move the universe.'

After Dilly's illness confined him to bed at home, leadership of the team was given to Peter Twinn, who had been at Bletchley Park from the first days in 1939. Twinn's first technical achievement at Bletchley had been on a different Enigma problem – that of the all-important Wehrmacht machine. Perhaps, though, a still greater achievement was to act as pilot for the mathematicians arriving at Bletchley Park. Twinn was the first, later saying, 'They regarded mathematicians as very strange beasts indeed, and required a little persuasion before they believed they could do anything practical or helpful at all.' Nevertheless, it was the success of mathematical techniques against that device that built the postwar reputation of Bletchley Park, and contributed hugely to the understanding of German military intentions during the conflict itself. Immediately before the war, the British – including Dilly Knox – had had very little understanding of the Wehrmacht Enigma machine. As reported by Christopher Morris, one of the codebreakers from King's College, Cambridge, Alastair Denniston said to Frank Birch one day in 1940, 'You know, the Germans don't mean you to read their stuff, and I don't suppose you ever will.' That was the challenge. To solve it would not just make the reputation of Bletchley Park, but it would make one of Bletchley's mathematicians a household name in future years. But to tell that story, it is necessary to rewind the clock.

Peter Twinn (1916–2004)

Peter Twinn was the first British cryptanalyst to read a German service message encrypted on an Enigma machine. Having learned from Dilly Knox the answer to the all-important question of the internal wiring of the Wehrmacht Enigma machine, Twinn was able to work out the wiring of the coding rotors and to begin to read a few old messages intercepted in 1938. It was of no military value, but as a leap forward in British capability it was immense.

Twinn was unusual for a GC&CS recruit in that he actually applied for the job early in 1939, by responding to an advertisement seeking mathematicians for government work. At the time he was doing a postgraduate course in Physics, having obtained a mathematics degree at Oxford. Twinn joined the GC&CS team studying Enigma before the move to Bletchley Park, and after the war began he worked closely with Knox and Turing on the machine methods which were needed for Enigma cryptanalysis. He said that Knox 'didn't believe in wasting too much time on training his assistant. He gave me a five-minute talk and told me to get on with it.'

After the war, Twinn transferred within the Civil Service to various other departments, including the Ministry of Technology and the Royal Aircraft Establishment. He also developed an interest in insect biology, using high-speed cameras to study the jumping of click beetles. That led to an awkward moment when military police apprehended Twinn on the runway at Farnborough. The story about collecting click beetles was too incredible for the policeman, who in turn was embarrassed to learn in due course that his prisoner was ultimately his boss.

As well as an entomologist, Peter Twinn was a musician, playing viola and clarinet. Through music at Bletchley he met his wife Rosamund, who was a cellist as well as a fellow Bletchley Park employee. He always downplayed his role in the Enigma break, saying that 'the job was little more than a routine operation.'

 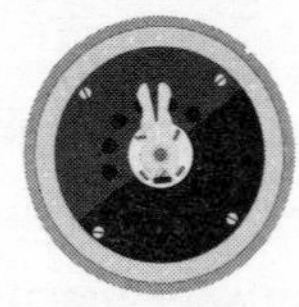 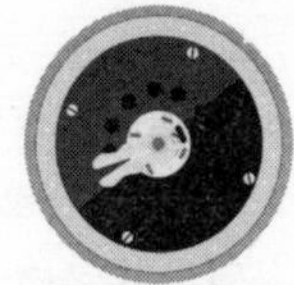

CHAPTER 4
The Bombe Squad

On 9 September 1938, Captain John Tiltman (see pages 133–6, Chapter 6) summed up the state of British knowledge on the Enigma problem. 'In 1931 we were provided by the French with photographs and directions for the use of the German Army Enigma Cipher Machine. The photographs show an attachment on the front of the machine which does not appear on the model available to the public… Can the French be asked to give us all the information they have with regard to the following points? (a) Full details of all devices additional to or differing from the market model. (b) What is the Army practice with regard to the following….' A longish list then followed. By the spring of the next year, the British at GC&CS were not much wiser; although the French were helpful, they did not know the answer to Captain Tiltman's questions. The problem was that without two crucial pieces of information the techniques painstakingly developed by Dilly Knox for attacking the Italian-Spanish Enigma machine during the Spanish Civil War were of no avail against the Germans.

The two things Knox was desperate to know were what the plugboard, shown in the photos, actually did, and secondly, how the wiring to the 'crown' connected up in the rest of the machine. The 'crown' was an electrical entry-plate – called by the French the *couronne fixe*, or the fixed crown – a circular set of electrical connections which led current from the keyboard into the bank of rotors. In the commercially-available machine referred to by Tiltman, pressing the Q key led current to the A connector in the crown, pressing W led to B, E to C and so forth. In the Wehrmacht machine a different wiring pattern was being used. There were 403,291,461,126,605,635,583,999,999 ways the Wehrmacht machine might be wired up if Q-A, W-B, E-C was not being used – rather more than anyone had time or patience to test one by one. This issue was called the 'QWERTZU', after the layout of letters on a German keyboard.

In fact, the British lack of understanding of Enigma's wiring was shown up by them naming the problem the 'QWERTZU'. The lettering on the keyboard was a side-issue, for the wiring didn't go straight from the keyboard to the crown, like the commercial machine: it went to the plugboard first. The crown-wiring problem was actually about how the crown was connected to the plugboard. Even so, a better understanding of the machine was the thing the British needed as Hitler's menacing moves turned into a full-scale occupation of Czechoslovakia and a tearing up of the Munich agreement in the spring of 1939. Despite cooperation with the French, that gap in GC&CS's knowledge continued right up to the summer.

Nous avons le QWERTZU, nous marchons ensemble!

Yet by September 1939, as German tanks rolled across Poland in the first demonstration of *blitzkrieg*, a new team under Knox had developed the basic design for a stunning piece of technology which would endure throughout the war and enable the British to break Enigma messages on a near-daily basis. How could the fortunes of Enigma codebreaking have become so utterly transformed in a matter of weeks, and at such a crucial juncture?

To answer this question, we have to turn back the clock still further. To be precise, to June 1931. A German man had walked into the French Embassy in Berlin and offered his services – services which included access to the documents explaining the operating procedures for the newly-adapted military version of the Enigma machine. The French, led by an intelligence officer called Gustave Bertrand, took the bait, paid handsomely for the papers (and a great deal of other intelligence which the man, code-named agent Asche, was to provide over the coming years) and then found, to their dismay, that their cipher experts could not squeeze out the vital information – the internal wiring of the machine – from the copies of the booklets they had acquired. The documents were then, as dutifully noted by Captain Tiltman, offered by Bertrand to the British, who also drew a blank. But the French had a third option – to offer the documents to the Polish, who were also allied. This time, the documents were accepted with great enthusiasm, although the French were kept in the dark about whether the Poles had got anything of value out of them.

As it turned out, the Polish team included a mathematician called Marian Rejewski who rapidly distilled the Enigma problem into a set of equations. They were no ordinary equations and were fiendish to solve. And even Marian Rejewski needed to know the answer to what Knox would later dub the QWERTZU. But Rejewski's approach to the QWERTZU was simple: he guessed that the Germans might have been unimaginative (or methodical) and chosen to wire Q to Q, W to W, E to E and so forth – and when he tried that out, his equations began to solve themselves in a way which seemed right. Rejewski then went on to reconstruct the wiring in the coding rotors, and thus he was able to replicate on paper the entire operation of the Enigma machine. From that point, in 1932, the Poles began working on various techniques and devices to determine how the Germans had set up their machines every day – what rotor order, which cross-pluggings, which ring-settings, and which rotor letter was uppermost.

The alliance with France, and by the end of the 1930s, with Britain, was developing meanwhile. The French coaxed MI6, and via MI6's second-in-command, Stewart Menzies, GC&CS into a three-way codes and ciphers alliance for sharing knowhow and intelligence on codebreaking, involving the experts from GC&CS, from France's *Deuxième Bureau*, and from Poland's *Biuro Szyfrów*. This began with a rather fruitless meeting in Paris in January 1939, but at least the

Marian Rejewski, the Polish mathematician who reverse-engineered the Enigma machine through the application of mathematical analysis.

codebreakers from the three countries had met each other. The Polish delegation was not yet authorized to divulge their breakthrough on the one question which the French and British wanted answered, which was the internal structure of the Enigma machine. Despite them having known it for over six years, the Poles were not telling – but they did agree that if 'something came up' they would call for another conference.

By mid-July the Poles realized that the threat from the Germans was intolerable. By drawing the French and British closer, the paper guarantee given by both those countries during the Czechoslovakia crisis could be converted into the real business of military cooperation; and to buy that, the Poles had a secret which they knew the British and the French wanted very badly. So, they sent a telegram: something had come up, and the other two delegations (Bertrand for the French, Denniston and Knox for the British) were invited to Warsaw to find out what.

To the astonishment of the guests, the Poles had done it all. Not only had Rejewski discovered the wiring – explaining to an incredulous Knox how he had done that – but the team, including codebreaker-mathematicians Jerzy Różycki and Henryk Zygalski and engineer-codebreaker Antoni Palluth, had invented a wondrous range of machines and paper methods for finding the daily Enigma settings. The Poles showed their allies the machines they had created and how they worked. They promised to send over a reconstructed Enigma machine to each of the two guest delegations (via the diplomatic bag). They explained everything.

An elated Knox – elated once he had recovered from his dismay at being trounced, for almost certainly the only time in his life, on an intellectual problem in which he was the expert – was heard saying '*Nous avons le QWERTZU – nous marchons ensemble*' (We have the QWERTZU, we go forward together). When, a few weeks later, the French team brought the reconstructed Enigma over from Paris, there was another outbreak of emotion. Menzies met the boat-train at Victoria station, wearing his rosette of the Légion d'Honneur in the buttonhole of his dinner-jacket. '*Accueil triomphal!*' (triumphal welcome) said Gustave Bertrand.

The Polish Quartet

Antoni Palluth (1900–44)
Marian Rejewski (1905–80)
Jerzy Różycki (1909–42)
Henryk Zygalski (1908–78)

Antoni Palluth bears the distinction of being the first Polish codebreaker – possibly the first codebreaker anywhere – to tackle the problem of Enigma. It was, in part, his failure that led to the decision to recruit mathematicians to the Polish Army's Cipher Bureau, beginning with an out-of-hours course to identify young potential cryptanalysts in Poznań in 1929.

The three who did best – Marian Rejewski, Jerzy Różycki and Henryk Zygalski – were hired, but only when the documents lifted by Hans-Thilo Schmidt became available was Rejewski let into the secret of the Enigma problem. Once he had reverse-engineered the machine, it was open to Palluth to build reconstructions and to the whole team to devise techniques to determine how the German armed forces were setting up their machines for use. Różycki and Zygalski excelled at this, and Palluth, who remained closely involved, brought the concepts into hardware form.

Once war broke out, the team needed to escape occupied Poland; despite the attempts of Denniston to bring the three mathematicians into the Bletchley Park team in 1940, none of them ever saw Bletchley Park, and only Rejewski and Zygalski lived long enough to see the greatest secret of World War II revealed to the public. Różycki and Palluth both died during the war.

The Letchworth connection

Armed now with the QWERTZU it was theoretically possible for the British to begin codebreaking, as Peter Twinn (see pages 87–8, Chapter 3) did soon after learning the details. But to break the enciphered messages in real time would require something like the Polish machine techniques for finding the settings currently in use by the German Enigma operators. And here was a new problem in the making.

The Polish techniques, and in particular their codebreaking machine called the *bomba*, depended on a German operating procedure which was likely to be discontinued. What they did was to signal to the receiver of a message, in a coded form, how the three rotors of the Enigma machine should be orientated for the start of the enciphered transmission. The code consisted of nothing more complicated than the three rotor-letters which were to be visible in the uppermost position at the starting point, twice over (in case of bad reception) and enciphered – using the Enigma machine. The Poles had exploited the twice-enciphered 'indicator' sequence in designing the *bomba*. But if the Germans identified the double-encipherment of the indicator as a security flaw, then they might stop the practice, and the *bomba* idea would be rendered useless overnight.

As soon as Knox got back from Warsaw, he wanted to check the mathematical approach explained by Rejewski, and to do that he consulted Twinn and another mathematician, one who was on the emergency professors list compiled by Alastair Denniston. That was Alan Turing, who had been working on and off on the Enigma problem ever since his induction course at GC&CS in January 1939. Turing reckoned it should be possible to develop the ideas behind the *bomba* into a new device which would not depend on double-encipherment of the three-letter indicator. Being familiar with Knox's methods using rods to find Enigma settings based on 'cribs', or guessed-at pre-encipherment message text, Turing took the electro-mechanical testing concept used in the *bomba* to invent a completely new machine, the bombe, named in honour of the boost given by the Poles to the British battle against Enigma.

Alan Turing (1912–54)

The story of Alan Turing has been told many times, though it tends to overstate his personal role in the breaking of Enigma at Bletchley Park. For many years he was known for his achievements in other fields – but when the story of Bletchley Park broke out, so did the story of Alan Turing.

In Turing's early years, his parents were stationed overseas in India, and their two children were boarded with a foster family in England. Here and at school, young Alan found that he could explore his interests in science and nature. He won a place at King's College, Cambridge, to study mathematics, finishing with the top grade (B-star wrangler) and a clutch of college rowing trophies.

It was while attending a course taught by M.H.A. Newman on foundations of mathematics that his first, and most lasting, breakthrough of genius came upon him. This was the idea of a programmable machine for computing – something which could vary its task according to the instructions it was fed. Not only did the concept (at the time, a purely theoretical idea) solve one of the great unknowns in mathematical theory, but it also founded a new discipline of mathematics now known as Computability. And, for non-specialists, it set out the theoretical foundation for all programmable computers which began to be built after World War II.

So, it is not surprising that, immediately upon the war's end, Turing was recruited by the National Physical Laboratory to produce a design for Britain's Automatic Computing Engine. The design was ready within a matter of months, but – unlike the execution of the bombe project – it took years for the machine to be built. (In fact, it did not become operational until some years after Turing's death.) Turing went on to design programming languages and to write programs; he also concluded that machines could be programmed to learn, writing a paper which was not published by the NPL for 20 years (again posthumously) because it was too fantastic. Turing also initiated a controversial debate on whether machines could think, and the famous 'imitation game' test, which continues to engage people today.

By the late 1940s Turing took a new job in the computing laboratory being established by Newman at the University of Manchester. There, Turing gradually moved away from computer design towards a new field of study: the shape and development of living things. He modelled the chemical processes which might be going on in plant and animal tissues, using the computer to predict the patterns found on animal skins and the points where branches emerge from plant stems.

In 1952 he was arrested for 'gross indecency' (gay sex in private). The outcome of the trial was that Turing was not sent to prison or fined but put on probation, with a condition that he submit to 'treatment', which included a course of synthetic oestrogen. By 1953 the course was over. Nevertheless, by the summer of 1954 he decided that he would end his life in his own way. It is inevitable that people link the conviction and the suicide, though the evidence for the one as cause of the other is tenuous.

After the story of Bletchley Park emerged, the name of Alan Turing became increasingly well-known. So much so, that a spate of Government initiatives to try to re-set the record has taken place: an official apology, and then a Royal Pardon, and in 2019 his selection to be the face of the £50 note. There have been biographies, plays, cantatas, sculptures and feature films and, in the centenary year of Alan Turing's birth, a vast number of conferences and symposia focused on the contribution of Alan Turing to academic thought – the thing for which he would, probably, most have wished to be remembered.

The essence of the bombe was that it would laboriously crank through all 17,576 possible positions of the three Enigma rotors, testing each one in turn to see if it was the starting point of the message which had been intercepted. If there was a starting point from which every letter in the crib could have become enciphered as per the intercept, the machine would stop, and – just maybe – one of the 150 million-million-million settings of the Enigma machine had been identified. But Turing's bombe machine went further than finding the possible starting-point for encryption: it also identified one of the cross-pluggings on the plugboard, and this made it much more powerful than its Polish predecessor.

The British Bombe (1940–59)

The British bombe was born out of the Polish *bomba*, which was designed to automate the drudgery of searching through thousands of possible settings to identify one plausible set-up of the rotors which might have been used for

Alan Turing, probably Bletchley Park's best-known codebreaker, whose electro-mechanical bombe machines found the daily Enigma settings.

encryption. Combining this electro-mechanical idea with the 'cribbing' technique used by Dilly Knox for his hand-based attack on Enigma made for a very powerful new generation of codebreaking machine.

During the peak of bombe machine production, one machine was being created at Letchworth every week. Over two hundred machines were made in Britain. Each contained 19 km (12 miles) of wire, was about 2 m (6½ ft) wide, nearly 2 m (6½ ft) tall, and 60 cm (2 ft) deep, weighing in at about a tonne (2,205 lb). The cost of each machine was equivalent to that of one-third of a Lancaster bomber. The machines needed a heavy duty electricity supply and constant maintenance because of their delicate moving parts.

There was a family of bombe designs, just as there were different types of Enigma machine. There were special bombes for the Abwehr Enigma traffic, high-speed four-rotor bombes for German Navy messages, and, towards the end of the war when a new model Enigma machine with a pluggable reflector plate threatened to come into operation, a monster machine which was effectively four bombes rigged to work together – appropriately named the Giant.

After the war ended, the need for bombe machines became questionable. Many were broken up, but not all. Apparently, some foreign agencies – notably, the East German secret police – continued to rely on Enigma for encrypting their secret communications. So, the technology was not obsolete just yet. Fifty British machines were kept by GCHQ, but by 1959 they had been out of use for some years and the survivors were also scrapped.

There is a sequel. In 1995, a retired engineer called John Harper began a project to reconstruct a bombe machine from a

A wartime photograph of a bombe machine, showing the banks of three 'drums' which replicated the behaviour of Enigma rotors.

patchwork of old drawings and records released to Bletchley Park by GCHQ. His persistence and dedication led to a rebuilt bombe coming into operation in 2007, more than 50 years after the previous bombe run. The rebuilt bombe can be seen working at the National Museum of Computing at Bletchley Park. (An American World War II four-rotor bombe, to a different design, still exists and can be viewed at the National Cryptologic Museum at Fort Meade, Maryland, though it doesn't work any more.)

So much for the concept. The next task was to try to turn an idea into engineering reality. Alan Turing was hardly the person to do this; once the engineering firm had been identified, the task fell to Peter Twinn. The chosen firm was the company which held the franchise for manufacturing and distributing IBM's 'Hollerith' punched-card machinery in Britain, the British Tabulating Machine Company in Letchworth, some 50km (30 miles) from Bletchley Park. BTM's chief engineer was Harold Keen (see pages 186 and 188–9, Chapter 8), known as 'Doc' because he carried his tools around in a doctor's bag. For the next six years, Doc Keen would be intimately involved in Britain's greatest secret: the machinery which would be used to break the Enigma cipher.

Starting in the autumn of 1939, Keen and Twinn began planning the design and development of the prototype British bombe. For reasons lost to history, their meetings took place at the White Hart Inn in Buckingham, where it was agreed that the British bombe would be constructed to behave like ten Enigma machines wired up together. (In fact, the standard bombe, as later created, had no fewer than 36 Enigma analogues.) At the heart of the machine were banks of three 'drums' – behaving exactly as Enigma rotors, with each set of three drums behaving like the rotors of an Enigma machine. Each bank of drums (called a 'Letchworth Enigma' at Bletchley) could be wired up at the back of the bombe machine to carry out the crib-test designed by Turing. With Keen's engineering skill, the bombe would be able to rattle through all 17,576 possible rotor positions in somewhat more than ten minutes. To achieve that, the drums had to have precision electrical contacts which would be broken and re-made as the drum rotated around the electrical contact points on the machine's housing. This was done with little wire brushes; if the brushes got bent when drums were taken off the machine, then the contacts would not work properly and the results would be wrong. (The female workforce of GC&CS who were deployed as bombe operators used to keep eyebrow tweezers to ensure the errant brushes were correctly aligned.)

The first week of April 1940 marked the beginning of the war in the West. German forces began their invasion of Norway, shortly followed by the Allied attempt to do the same thing. By the end of the month, the British had begun a withdrawal. It was not a glorious moment for the Allied forces. But Keen's prototype bombe became ready for delivery during the same month, and in Hut 1 at Bletchley Park it was put through its paces.

As with the Norwegian campaign, there was a lot to learn. The problem with Alan Turing's bombe was that it stopped all the time. Stops were, in theory, a good thing: the machine stopped when it found a plausible rotor combination which deserved further investigation. But too many stops meant too much further testing. The problem could be circumvented with very clever wiring patterns, connecting the sets of 'Letchworth Enigmas' into circular loops, but it was very difficult to get a crib/intercept combination which allowed for those patterns. Perhaps the Turing bombe idea was a flop.

Actually, it wasn't a total failure, being able to break some naval settings in May and June, but hand methods for tackling Enigma were more efficient at producing results during these months. Something needed to happen urgently on the solution of Enigma, since the Germans had changed their methods on 1 May. On that day they stopped using the twice-enciphered indicator sequence which had been exploited so successfully by the Poles. At a stroke, the old techniques were obsolete. Turing's bombe needed a radical improvement, since the hand methods depended on German operator errors which – while prevalent – could not be guaranteed to produce high volumes of decrypts with reliability.

The diagonal board

It wasn't diagonal, nor was it a board, but it was certainly brilliant. Gordon Welchman, a Cambridge mathematician who had been 'banished' to the school-block behind Bletchley Park on his arrival, was not completely out of the loop on the Enigma problem. He had been working on call signs and the message preambles, which enabled messages to be sorted according to the network on which they originated and therefore shared a common Enigma set-up. He was also watching the bombe project with interest. One day it dawned on him that more loops – the electrical circuits needed to make Alan Turing's bombe easier to wire up, and to stop less often – could be created using a simple additional piece of electrical engineering: the diagonal board.

Welchman's idea for a 'diagonal board' was based on the basic fact that everyone knew about Enigma machines: it was reciprocal. If the sender of a message keyed in **A** and the light for **Z** lit up, that meant that when the receiver of the message keyed in **Z** the light for **A** must light up in the decoding process. So, on the plugboard, any pair of cross-pluggings was also reciprocal: **Q** plugged to **K** meant that **K** was also plugged to **Q**. The diagonal board reproduced reciprocity in electrical form: if the electrical test being done by the bombe machine was trying out a cross-plugging in one direction (Q→K) it should simultaneously test the other direction (K→Q). Welchman showed his idea to Turing, drawing it out as a panel, or board, in two dimensions with wires crossing diagonally. Turing was initially dumbfounded, but quickly recognized that this was just the improvement which the bombes needed.

Gordon Welchman (1906–85)

Alan Turing and Gordon Welchman might not appear to have too much in common: Turing was gay, Welchman definitely not; Welchman was a well-organized and capable manager, Turing definitely not; Welchman sufficiently fond of America to become a US citizen, while Turing reportedly 'hated' America; and so on.

But in a piece called 'Ultra Revisited', written in 1983, Gordon Welchman found some curious parallels in their lives. Both were Cambridge mathematicians. Both were intimately connected with the invention of the bombe machine which found the daily settings used by the Germans to encipher

Gordon Welchman, mathematician, co-designer of the bombe, and later head of the machine co-ordination section at Bletchley Park.

Enigma messages; both were given the OBE for their work at Bletchley. Both were deprived of their security clearance in the postwar period for reasons which, to each of them at the time, seemed absurd.

Welchman joined Bletchley Park in the wave of professor-types who arrived in the first days of September 1939. He was put onto traffic analysis in a school building behind the main Bletchley Park buildings, but soon realized that plenty of information could be gleaned from what would today be called 'metadata' sent along with messages that were indecipherable. He was loosely associated with the Enigma team and thereby made his great contribution to the efficiency of the bombe.

Perhaps his greatest contribution at Bletchley was on the administrative side: as head of Hut 6, the Army and Air Force ciphers section; and as head of the Machine Co-ordination and Development Section established in 1943. It was Welchman's initiative that caused Bletchley Park to be organized into an efficient structure, from which the seamless delivery of intelligence could be achieved from a mass of decrypts – an idea which may have seemed absurd in the early days of the war when solving Enigma was still an untried gamble and many officers thought that radio silence would be imposed during major operations.

After the war, Welchman did not go back to Cambridge but joined the John Lewis Partnership management, before moving to the United States to work for the MITRE corporation, an offshoot of MIT which advised on secret defence initiatives. After the story of Bletchley Park's wartime achievements began to emerge in the 1970s, Welchman wrote his own account of Enigma codebreaking, *The Hut Six Story*, and was condemned by the British for doing so, since (even at the distance of 40 years) it was considered a gross breach of the Official Secrets Act. For this sin he was deprived of his security clearance and no longer able to work at MITRE.

The amount of equipment needed for this additional thing, the diagonal board, was trivial: Doc Keen wound the cross-wirings into a single skein which fitted neatly at the side of the bombe. So it ended up looking more like a long, straight plait of hair than a diagonal board, but so what. The new bombe machine was called 'Aggie', short for Agnus Dei, and it arrived in Hut 1 on 8 August 1940. France had fallen, the invasion of Britain was imminent, but the improved machine worked. Instantly it was finding settings of German Air Force Enigma machines. It was just in time: the air war over Britain began in earnest on 10 August, with 1,485 German aircraft attacking three days later. The following day, Bletchley Park decrypts told Winston Churchill that Germany would not invade until air superiority had been obtained. Enigma decrypts, courtesy of the bombe, were beginning to show their mettle.

Winston Churchill was hugely interested in the secret intelligence which emanated from Bletchley Park. If knowledge is power, Churchill knew how to convert the one to the other. Equipped with the special delivery of decrypts from Bletchley which he received every day from Stewart Menzies, who became head of the Secret Intelligence Service (MI6) shortly after the outbreak of war, Churchill was able to bombard his entourage with unexpected facts and thereby to win an argument. Churchill visited Bletchley on 6 September 1941, going around the huts to give pep talks to the codebreakers. W.F. Clarke recounted the visit with his characteristic splash of sarcasm:

Winston made us a very nice speech of thanks and went off to lunch at Blenheim. He had arrived in the usual cortège of cars with flags

> *flying and must have been spotted by the local inhabitants. For lunch, the BP staff crowded out into the town and no doubt talked about the visit to all and sundry. Late that afternoon, an order came round to say that his visit must be kept secret.*

A visit from Mr Churchill was nonetheless good for morale – except that things were not quite as perfect as the prime ministerial presence might have implied. The Enigma project was the star achievement of Bletchley Park, but in 1941 it was grossly under-resourced.

The wicked uncles

It was the grossest breach of protocol, a violation of reporting lines, an act of military disobedience of court-martial proportions, and it was impolite. Fortunately for the perpetrators, they were not in the navy and their service superior was Commander Denniston, whose naval commission was in the Volunteer Reserve – in other words, he was a civilian in uniform. Yet to reach around him, over his head, to go to the very top with a letter of complaint, took a deal of rule breaking and courage which might be unexpected from a bunch of professors working on obscure problems in cryptanalysis.

> *Hut 6 and Hut 8, Bletchley Park.*
> *21 October 1941.*
>
> Dear Prime Minister,
>
> Some weeks ago you paid us the honour of a visit, and we believe that you regard our work as important. You will have seen that, thanks largely to the energy and foresight of Commander Travis, we have been well supplied with the 'bombes' for the breaking of the German Enigma codes. We think, however, that you ought to know that this work is being held up, and in some cases is not being done at all, principally because we cannot get sufficient staff to deal with it. Our reason for writing to you direct is that for months we have done everything that we possibly can

> through the normal channels, and that we despair of any early improvement without your intervention…
>
> We are, Sir, Your obedient servants,
>
> A.M. Turing W.G. Welchman
> C.H.O'D. Alexander P.S. Milner-Barry

The wicked thing was being done, and in doing it the four servants needed to be disobedient. The letter had to be delivered, and the consequences faced. There was no point in trying to send the letter via the internal Civil Service mail, for Denniston or one of his administration staff would have asked awkward questions and the initiative lost. Personal delivery was needed. The business of getting a letter to Number 10, Downing Street, was simple: Milner-Barry, the youngest of the conspirators, would take the train to London. Getting past the front door of Number 10 was perhaps less simple. The guard dog was Brigadier George Harvie-Watt, the PM's principal private secretary, who quite rightly said that no one without an appointment could enter. Milner-Barry could not even produce an official ID to explain who he was, but refused to divulge to anyone other than the addressee what the contents contained: who could tell whether Harvie-Watt or indeed anyone at Downing Street was cleared for this particular secret? It was a stand-off.

Harvie-Watt must have been used to odd civilians turning up on secret missions, so the letter was put on Churchill's desk. Churchill read the letter, and scrawled on it 'Let these people have everything they want on extreme priority and report to me that this has been done.' Also on Churchill's desk was a pile of red paper tabs, each printed with the words ACTION THIS DAY. One of those was pinned to the letter, and Churchill's beleaguered Chief of the Imperial General Staff, General Ismay, found himself with one more task.

Back at Bletchley, life seemed to carry on as normal. Milner-Barry and the other three authors, later known as 'the wicked uncles', didn't get fired. Maybe the letter hadn't got through? In any case, there was a war to win. The enemy, if not a shortage of resources, was the enemy at sea: Naval Enigma.

The Wicked Uncles

Sir Stuart Milner-Barry (1906–95)
Hugh Alexander (1909–74)

It is a curious thing that the deputies of Alan Turing (Hut 8 – Naval codes) and Gordon Welchman (Hut 6 – Army and Air force codes) had so much in common. Furthermore, Alexander was older than his notional boss, Turing, and Milner-Barry was the same age as his, Welchman. This made for rather informal organizational arrangements, and probably contributed to the success of Bletchley Park.

Milner-Barry met Alexander in 1924 at the schoolboy chess championships, when Alexander stole the crown from Milner-Barry. Alexander was probably the better player, going on to become British champion in 1938, play for England, and write books about chess, but it was Milner-Barry who was chess correspondent for the *Times* newspaper. Being old friends, they shared digs for the whole of their time at Bletchley Park.

For both of them, Bletchley Park was a release from prewar jobs they disliked: stockbroking in the case of Milner-Barry, and an administrative job with John Lewis for Alexander ('he was far too untidy even to look like a businessman'). Both arrived in early 1940, when Gordon Welchman's Hut system was coming into being, both joining Hut 6. By 1941 work on the Naval Enigma problem, led by Alan Turing, needed more organizational as well as creative talent, so Alexander moved across, and by the mid-part of 1942 was effectively in charge of

Hut 8. By 1943, when both Turing and Welchman had moved to new roles, Milner-Barry was leading Hut 6, and Alexander's position had been confirmed.

After the war, Milner-Barry stayed in the Civil Service, working for most of his career in the Treasury and emerging from service with a knighthood. He defended Gordon Welchman when he came under fire for publishing his own detailed account of Enigma codebreaking. Alexander went back to John Lewis briefly, but joined GCHQ in 1946, where he worked until his retirement. He too took on a defence role: when Alan Turing was prosecuted for gross indecency in 1952, Alexander appeared as a character witness, saying that his former boss was a 'national asset'.

Naval Enigma was more difficult than Army and Air Force Enigma because the 'indicator' system was more secure and much harder to unpick. Alan Turing had discovered the technique being used quite early on in the war, and at the time of the letter to Churchill he had become the head of Hut 8, the cryptanalytical unit dedicated to Naval Enigma's many problems. What Turing and Hut 8 needed was a way to solve the special indicator system which was being used by the U-boats.

By the beginning of 1942 it was becoming clear that putting Turing in charge of a Hut was not a wise decision. It was an administrative hangover from the old days, when people like Knox were nominated by Denniston to oversee, in a very loose way, the various researchers gathered around him. Hut 8 needed a more military, or more corporate type of organization; in fact, it just needed organization, and someone like Turing was not going to get around to organizing anything.

There are many stories of Turing's eccentricities – in a 1959 account, his mother recounted this one:

In the shelter during air raids he knitted himself a pair of gloves, with no pattern to guide him, just out of his head; he was, however, defeated when it came to completion of the fingers, so he used to bicycle in from Shenley with little tails of wool dangling from his fingertips until one of the girls in his office took pity on him and closed up the ends.

Sometimes, the laugh was on the other side:

I was informed that a Professor Turing was to be attached to us for a while on special duties and I arranged for his accommodation both in the mess and also in a hut. In spite of having to live in a mess and with soldiers, Turing soon settled down and became 'one of us' in every sense.... I well remember when we were arranging some sports in connection with a fête we were running, officers were asked to put up their names for any of the races. Imagine our surprise when Turing put his name up for the mile. We rather thought it might be a leg-pull, but on the Day 'The Prof.', by which name Turing was also known, came in a very easy first.

While Alan Turing's future role was being considered, the action commanded by Churchill was beginning to happen. From the grand total of two bombe machines in 1940, by the end of 1941 Bletchley had six with another ten at a couple of nearby manor houses, which had been taken over as outstations. In 1942 the number of bombes grew threefold, and more outstations were created. One, at Stanmore, grew into a huge facility housing 75 bombes; and in 1943 another enormous bombe complex was opened at Eastcote, where no fewer than 103 bombes were in operation by the time the war in Europe was over. (Eastcote also became the postwar home of GCHQ.)

Alongside the growth in bombe numbers it was necessary to grow the number of staff available to operate them. This implied some degree of specialism: it was hardly appropriate for the likes of Turing and

Welchman to spend their day tweaking wires and coaxing machinery into life, nor to have them sitting around waiting for bombe-runs to stop and to read out possible message settings. A new recruitment drive was needed, and this time the Navy was coming to the rescue.

'Free a man for the fleet' was the slogan used to bring women into the Royal Navy, specifically the Women's Royal Naval Service, or Wrens. On 24 March 1941 the first contingent, consisting of eight Wrens, arrived at Bletchley Park to operate bombes. As the need grew, many more young women were brought in to do the job. How disappointing it was for those who had hoped to travel, to smell the sea, and to meet dashing sailors – when they were assigned to HMS *Pembroke V*, only to discover that this was the Naval cover name for 'special duties' at Bletchley, which meant a role of mind-numbing boredom in dark, smelly, noisy proximity to bombes, and where the majority of one's work colleagues were other young women who were just as disillusioned.

Gwen Acason's experience at Bletchley began in 1944, when she was sent to Wavendon House, where some of the Wrens were accommodated. 'The only glimpse of water was a small lake in the grounds.' The next day 'found us boarding a bus transport which deposited us at some iron gates guarded by soldiers, in the town of Bletchley. Here we were told to alight and were ushered into a room where a Wren Officer addressed us. We were informed that we had been vetted by security and would be doing work of a highly secret nature and must sign the Official Secrets Act. Any mention of our work outside our office would bring dire punishment.'

A similar experience was that of Brenda Abrahams, who volunteered as soon as she was old enough to leave school. She was assigned to *Pembroke V*, and after three weeks of training, consisting mainly of marching and learning naval jargon (very useful for a future bombe operator) she was posted to the outstation at Stanmore. 'Conditions at Stanmore seemed to be permanently cold. The workplace where the bombes were kept was cold and we had only the hot smelly bombes to warm us up. The bays in which we slept were also very cold. In fact, it was so cold that whenever anyone was able to have a bath at the end of the bay, the bay itself would fill up with steam.'

Another Wren was Anne Pease, who came to Bletchley Park in August 1941. 'We were taken into the house and had to sign the Official Secrets Act, then taken over to Hut 11 where we saw all these amazing machines. I remember the noise and smell of them. It was very strange. Hut 11 was dark and very noisy with no natural light and there was the smell of engine oil. It really was terribly noisy. It had a sort of whirring noise with all wheels going round at once and then there was a clunk when it stopped.' Later on, Anne Pease was sent to the outstation at Wavendon House, a few miles from Bletchley, and at the end of the war she was posted to Colombo in Ceylon (now Sri Lanka). So, for a very few, joining the navy did allow you to see the world.

By the end of the war, over 2,600 Wrens were involved in codebreaking, either at Bletchley or one of the outstations. Not all of them worked on bombes and the breaking of Enigma – there were other codes to break and other tasks to perform. But for most of the Wrens the work itself was drudgery, and being secret the significance of what they were doing was barely known. Ruth Bourne, who operated bombes during the war, has spoken several times about her experiences. She joined the bombe team aged 18. After signing the Official Secrets Act, she was told her work involved codebreaking, but: 'I never even heard the name Enigma until long after the war. We didn't know anything about how the bombe worked or how it related to the Enigma machine. I was just putting wheels on and taking them off and putting plugs in and so on.'

Occasionally the Wrens were thanked for their help, but it was rare, and, in Ruth Bourne's recollection, even at home not everyone was impressed: 'Thirty years after the war ended, a man called Fred Winterbotham (see page 244, Chapter 10) wrote a book called *The Ultra Secret*, and that told that we had broken Enigma. I remember telling my husband, "Oh, this is what I did during the war, look, it's in the book, I broke codes." And he said, "Oh, that's interesting, dear, very interesting. What's for tea?"'

CCR 1
102(1)
65/4/7A

~~TOP SECRET ULTRA~~

I. A description of the machine.

We begin by describing the 'unsteckered enigma'. The machine consists of a box with 26 keys labelled with the letters of the alphabet and 26 bulbs which shine through stencils on which letters are marked. It also contains wheels whose function will be described later on. When a key is depressed the wheels are made to move in a certain way and a current flows through the wheels to one of the bulbs. The letter which appears over the bulb is the result of enciphering the letter on the depressed key with the wheels in the position they have when the bulb lights.

To understand the working of the machine it is best to separate in our minds

The electric circuit of the machine without the wheels.

The circuit through the wheels.

The mechanism for turning the wheels and for describing the positions of the wheels.

The circuit of the machine without the wheels.

Fig 1

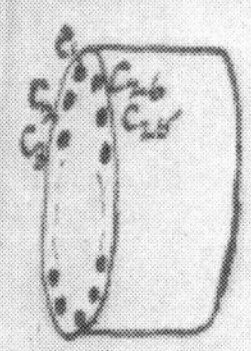

Eintrittswalz

The machine contains a cylinder called the Eintrittswalz (E.W) on which are 26 contacts $C_1, \ldots, C_{26}$. The effect of the wheels is to connect these contacts up in pairs, the actual pairings of course depending on the positions of the wheels. On the other side the contacts $C_1, C_2, \ldots, C_{26}$ are connected each to one of the keys. For the moment we will suppose that the order is QWERTZUIOASDFGHJKPYXCVBNML , and we will say that Q is the letter associated with C_1, W that associated with C_2 etc. This series of letters associated with $C_1, C_2, \ldots, C_{26}$

The beginning of the 'Treatise on the Enigma' written by Alan Turing to introduce recruits to the Enigma problem; it was commonly known as 'Prof's Book'.

Still, in 2018, the French Government honoured Ruth Bourne by making her a chevalier of the Légion d'Honneur for her contribution to the liberation of France in 1944.

The dull life of the bombe operator was an essential part of the overall success story of Enigma codebreaking. But the Wrens would not have been at Bletchley Park, operating machines being turned out by the BTM factory in their hundreds, without a revolutionary change from the prewar days of GC&CS and the 'men of the Professor type'. Something had happened, and as is the way of things, the revolution had claimed its victim.

 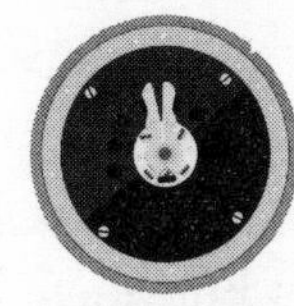 

CHAPTER 5
The Fall of Denniston

1941 was a rough year for Alastair Denniston. In February, he was diagnosed with a stone in his bladder. He was operated on in March but there were complications which emerged the following month and he was kept away from Bletchley Park until the last week of May. The hospital bills which followed were almost as painful as the condition and its treatment. Meanwhile, Bletchley Park had been governed by Commander Edward Travis, Denniston's deputy.

The Park itself was doing well in 1941: the difficult problem of Naval Enigma seemed to have found a solution, with a period of improving fortunes in the Atlantic U-boat war being the dividend, and with Army and Air Force Enigma making a mark in the intensifying conflict in North Africa. On another front, an intelligence relationship with the United States – still notionally neutral – was being constructed in slow steps. Denniston himself visited America twice in August 1941, each time taking the uncomfortable option of flying despite recording 'neuritis returns' in his diary between the trips. Denniston's emollient style was just what was needed to help overcome distrust and reluctance on both sides.

Alastair Denniston (1881–1961)

Alastair Denniston was the only person to have led GCHQ (or its predecessor) in the first 90 years of its existence and not to receive a knighthood. He is played by the actor Charles Dance in the movie *The Imitation Game* (which is about Enigma codebreaking and Alan Turing at Bletchley Park) and the portrayal is unrecognizable. The character which Dance is asked to play is a stern, unimaginative, unforgiving naval officer straight off the quarterdeck. The real-life Denniston could not have been more different, even if the scriptwriter had been paid a bonus to try.

We have to look further; and the controversy which still surrounds Denniston's removal from the leading role at Bletchley Park makes the search harder. Evidently Denniston was liked more than admired – 'My father's ability to make friends with his close colleagues was a major factor in his management style, and ultimately in the success of his undertakings,' wrote his son Robin – whereas Denniston's successor Edward Travis inspires comments in the opposite sense.

So, what are the facts? Alastair Denniston was not even named 'Alastair' – the 'A' stood for Alexander, but the reasons for him being called something else are lost. His father was a Scottish doctor, but died when Alastair was ten. Denniston developed an aptitude for languages, studying at London, Paris and Bonn, and in 1907 he took up a teaching post in Edinburgh; he was also a keen and successful sportsman, playing hockey for Scotland in his youth (achieving a bronze medal in the 1908 Olympics), cricket at Osborne, and golf for the whole of his life.

In 1909 he was recruited by the Royal Naval College at Osborne, on the Isle of Wight, as a civilian language teacher. It was that role that brought him into the sphere of Professor Alfred Ewing, the founder of Room 40, and thus into Room 40 itself as one of Ewing's first recruits. From Room 40, to

GC&CS, to Bletchley Park and ultimately to Berkeley Street and diplomatic codes, Denniston's career was settled.

After World War II, Denniston found himself on the beach. GC&CS was re-amalgamated into GCHQ, with Sir Edward Travis at the helm, and Denniston was pensioned off on 1 May 1945. He went back into teaching, finding that his official pension was somewhat meagre. After 30 years, he could be forgiven for his bitterness about the service which he had nurtured. In 2012, the then-director of GCHQ, Sir Iain Lobban, made the effort to redress the balance, describing Denniston's recruitment of Turing and Welchman as 'a crucial insight', and finding in his record inspiration for future directors of GCHQ in identifying 'a new type of cryptanalyst for a new era.'

Distrust and bickering were rife at Bletchley Park as well. Angry memos were flying around, and they were not being written by Dilly Knox, who by this time was working at home as his own illness had taken over. 'It was evident that the whole situation was getting out of hand and that GC&CS was apparently unable to control it,' recorded Nigel de Grey. Then, following the direct action taken by the 'wicked uncles' in their letter to Churchill, there were aftershocks. Many years later, Sir Stuart Milner-Barry wrote about it all:

> *The flow of bombes was speeded up, the staff bottlenecks were relieved, and we were able to devote ourselves uninterruptedly to the business in hand. Nor were there any serious thunderbolts from on high, other than a visitation on Hut 6 from 'C' (Stewart Menzies) who rebuked Gordon [Welchman] … for having 'wasted 15 minutes of the Prime Minister's time'. I by chance met Commander Denniston*

Alastair Denniston when he was still in control at Bletchley Park.

in the corridors some days later, and he made some rather wry remark about our unorthodox behaviour; but he was much too nice a man to bear malice.

In after years when I became a Whitehall bureaucrat conditioned to going through the proper channels, I looked back from time to time ... The thought of going straight from the bottom to the top would have filled my later self with horror and incredulity. And I wondered too what would have happened if the letter had not been written, and if the Prime Minister had not 'wasted 15 minutes of his time' in reading it.

Colonel Menzies, the head of MI6 and Denniston's superior, had not been amused by the way he had been made to look foolish in front of his main customer, Winston Churchill. In fact, notwithstanding Milner-Barry's failure to observe the thunderbolts, Menzies was furious. After Gordon Welchman's dressing-down, it was Denniston's turn. Menzies needed to ensure that this kind of nonsense never happened again – and it was clear that the reason for the gross dereliction of loyalty was that something was seriously amiss with the organization and management of Bletchley Park. To quote the official historian, 'the spate of argument and recrimination was damaging efficiency and threatening a breakdown of discipline'. One might be forgiven for thinking that discipline had already broken down.

Menzies initiated an enquiry, to be carried out by Major-General K.J. Martin, a former deputy director of military intelligence. Separately, following infighting in Hut 3, an investigation into organizational issues was going on about Hut 3 as well, led by a civilian in RAF uniform called Eric Jones (see pages 223–4, Chapter 9). Jones' report, identifying the 'background and structure of the GC&CS' as the root of the Hut 3 problem, was delivered on 2 February 1942. The results of Menzies' enquiry in January 1942 led to a second set of recommendations which was presented on 30 January. Both reports were clear. A shake-up of how Bletchley Park was run was unavoidable.

Der Führer takes charge

3 February 1942

Reorganization of GC&CS

With the ever-increasing work, I have found it necessary to carry out a reorganization of the GC&CS. The posts of Head of the GC&CS and Deputy Head of the GC&CS have been abolished and the work of the GC&CS will henceforth be divided into two parts: Civil [and] Services. Commander Denniston and Commander Travis are appointed Deputy Directors to control the Civil and Services' sides respectively.[8]

Behind the excuse for the reorganization, the imperative was to provide a better, more efficient service to support the armed forces in time of war. Things had changed since 1914–18: the variety, volume and complexity of the code and cipher traffic coming in from all fronts was enormous. Gone were the days of a super diplomatic coup such as the Zimmermann Telegram having major strategic impact across the world. Now it was all about getting the messages decoded, getting them sifted into intelligence, and getting the product out in time to make a difference. This needed a military mindset and the qualities of organization and command which come naturally to a commanding officer.

Alastair Denniston had never been a commanding officer: he had come into the Volunteer Reserve of the Royal Navy during World War I, when it was thought appropriate to give commissions to those serving in Room 40. Even Dilly Knox was a commissioned officer in the RNVR. Denniston had started out as a teacher, and it was his calm and modest style of management which enabled him to keep Knox and the professors in some kind of line. 'After twenty years' experience in GC&CS, I think I may say to you that one does not

8 Memo by Sir Stewart Menzies, National Archives of the United Kingdom.

expect to find the rigid discipline of a battleship among the collection of somewhat unusual civilians who form GC&CS.' Denniston wrote that to Oliver Strachey in 1940. By December 1941, such an approach to management was outmoded and failing. The new, mechanical era of codebreaking needed exactly what Denniston decried. It needed a battleship commander.

It was noteworthy that E.W. Travis had been singled out for praise by the wicked uncles – not the head of GC&CS, Alastair Denniston. Travis had a genuine navy background, and the temperament for commanding a large ship. He had clearly made a good showing when deputing for Denniston during Denniston's sickness in the spring of 1941.

Sir Edward Travis (1888–1956)

Sir Edward Travis became the first director of GCHQ when it was re-established under that name following World War II. During the war, he had been the prime force ensuring that Bletchley Park was well-resourced, well-run and effective, first as Alastair Denniston's deputy and, after the reorganization of 1942, as its head. Travis' management style owed something to his background in the Royal Navy, and while he was gruff and direct, his ability to get things done and to iron out the common-room squabbles which tended to bubble up among the codebreakers won him respect, if not affection, from across his vast empire.

Travis joined the Royal Navy on leaving school in 1906. On the outbreak of World War I, he was appointed as signals officer on the staff of Admiral Jellicoe. He transferred to the Admiralty in 1916, with responsibility for security of codes and ciphers, a responsibility which he continued between the

Sir Edward Travis, who took over the command of Bletchley Park in 1942.

wars when he joined the new GC&CS. He was appointed as Denniston's deputy in 1925, and by 1938 he was in charge of all the services' decryption work, including ultimate responsibility for the Enigma problem and the machine response to the challenge. It was Travis who was present when the prototype bombe in Hut 1 achieved its first 'stop' (its output of suggested Enigma settings) and took the details back to Turing and his Hut 8 team. It was also Travis who spearheaded the adoption of the secure version of the British cipher machine Typex, which resisted German attempts at codebreaking throughout the war.

Organization and administration may be less glamorous than triumphant breakthroughs on cipher systems widely thought to be unbreakable. Yet it was Travis' reorganization of GC&CS which enabled the codebreaking successes developed under Denniston's softer form of leadership to develop into an efficient machine which delivered the intelligence needed by the armed services quickly and effectively. His memos were signed in a distinctive brown ink, known as 'the Director's blood'. Following the war, his talents were needed to transition GCHQ to the new challenge of the Cold War, which he oversaw until his retirement in 1952. By that time (among other honours) Travis had been made a chevalier of the Légion d'Honneur (1919), an OBE (1936) and a KCMG (1944).

Menzies' memo about the reorganization tried to make it look as if Denniston and Travis were being given equal roles in the new world. But it was obvious to everyone that the Services division was the relevant and powerful one. At Bletchley Park the team working on diplomatic codes and ciphers was small – 80 or so staff – and something of a poor relation. Of course, during the previous war, 'diplomatic' had had far-reaching results; and as it turned out Denniston's new division, based at Berkeley Street in London and camouflaged by a ladies' hat shop, grew to around 200 people (more than the total complement of the GC&CS before World War II began) breaking codes from dozens of countries, notably including Germany, Japan, Italy and Vichy France. It is difficult to assess the full significance of the Civil Division of the GC&CS, even now, as some things remain to be declassified and the more popular Services work of Bletchley Park has overshadowed that of its cousin.

The reaction at Bletchley to the change was mixed. Those who had worked with Denniston closely for many years were, understandably, dismayed by what appeared to be a demotion. Denniston was highly regarded for 'his willingness to delegate, his trust in subordinates, his informality and his charm'.[9] It was, after all, under Denniston's leadership that the recruitment of the 'men of the Professor type' had happened, and it was evident that the infusion of intellect and innovation they had brought was the engine of Bletchley's successes. He had also sponsored the meetings with the Polish codebreakers which had led to the development of the bombe, a project which he had supported and encouraged.

Others, though, recognized the need for the change at the top. W.F. Clarke had been sceptical all along, observing that one of their colleagues had 'flatly declined to serve under Denniston' in 1919, noting that Denniston was 'described as possibly fit to manage a small sweet shop in the East End.' That was probably going too far, but Peter Twinn, architect of the bombe project, commented of Denniston, 'I do not regard him as a success', and Stuart Milner-Barry, one of the wicked uncles, said that by 1940 Denniston was a 'busted flush'. Still others thought there had been a palace plot, with Travis telling Menzies that Denniston had to go or he would resign

---

9 F. H. Hinsley, 'Alastair Denniston' in *The Oxford Dictionary of National Biography*.

himself, supported by Nigel de Grey (who became Travis's number two at Bletchley) and Frederic Freeborn (see pages 191–2, Chapter 8), the head of the machine section on whom much depended.

Travis, described by Welchman as a 'bulldog of a man', was nicknamed 'der Führer' for his more robust style of command, at least by those who were brave enough. The acid W.F. Clarke, lingering on at Bletchley, noted how unsuitable it was for de Grey to refer to Travis as 'our beloved chief', but even he noted that Travis 'was always very nice to me'. From the spring of 1942, under Travis, Bletchley Park began to work like a military operation, with clear lines of command and clear allocation of priorities. Travis would now have an opportunity to develop the ideas which he, together with Gordon Welchman, had been trying to implement since the early days of 1940. Bletchley Park was set to become an intelligence factory.

It was just in time: 1942 was the year when what Churchill called 'the hinge of fate' had begun to turn. Just as the Americans entered the war, the war in the North Atlantic had worsened: U-boats were sinking merchant shipping at unprecedented rates. The Germans had adopted a new form of Enigma machine for communication between the U-boats and their shore command. Worse, the Germans were reading Allied codes. The convoys should have been hidden by the ocean's sheer size, but the Germans knew from reading British coded messages where the convoys were. And that was not all of it. Intelligence reports sent from Cairo by the US military attaché back to Washington were being intercepted, decoded, and sent to Rommel in the North African desert: he had an up-to-the-moment appreciation, from the best of sources, of exactly what the British order of battle was, the availability of men and matériel, and the state of their morale. If Bletchley Park was going to win the battle of the secret airwaves, it would have to be in 1942.

  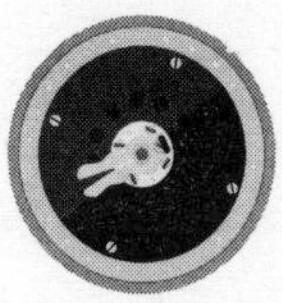

CHAPTER 6
The Hut-dwellers

When Gordon Welchman arrived at Bletchley Park, he was assigned to work with Dilly Knox. Knox was not an easy taskmaster: 'certainly during my first week or two at Bletchley I got the impression he didn't like me.... Anyway, very soon after my arrival I was turned out of the Cottage and set to Elmers School, where I was to study "callsigns and discriminants," groups of letters and figures which were a regular feature in the preambles of German Enigma messages.' Welchman was not impressed. First of all, Elmers School was behind the main Bletchley site, and secondly the study of preambles hardly seemed to be a war-winning occupation. Actually, Welchman soon realized he was wrong about all this.

In 1939, when Welchman was enduring the 'banishment' (his word) to the empty school, Bletchley Park was in the beginnings of a transformation from a pseudo-stately home to a work site. All over the gardens, wooden huts were being knocked together to form additional working space for the extra staff which kept arriving. And Welchman discovered, from his study of discriminants and preambles, that he could figure out a great deal about the way the German military radio service was organized, and that led him to some conclusions about the way Bletchley Park was itself organized.

The four huts

The autumn of 1939 was the period of the 'Phoney War', where nothing much was happening, at least as far as the war on land and in the air was concerned. Yet there were still plenty of Enigma messages swimming about the ether: so many, in fact, that there were not enough interceptors to capture all the traffic. If and when the war turned into a hot war, the volume was likely to increase dramatically. Even assuming no codebreaking was possible, the intelligence derived from the preambles and call signs alone would be valuable and deserved an increase in staff. Furthermore, if you assumed – and Welchman was ready to assume this, in light of his own contribution to the bombe machine project – that Enigma messages could be broken, there would need to be a full-scale decoding room and a proper system for handling the deciphered messages, translating them, and evaluating their content.

'With considerations such as these in mind, I formulated an organizational plan and took it to Commander Edward Travis, deputy director, under Alastair Denniston, of all Bletchley Park activities.' The plan was this: there should be a system for registering intercepts, and carrying out the traffic analysis which Welchman had been doing in the school; there should be close liaison with the 'Y' service, which picked up the radio messages, to help them prioritize their work; there should be a cryptanalysis department, devoted to finding out the 'key' (Enigma settings) which the Germans were using; and there should be a decoding department, which would strip away the Enigma cipher once the key was known, and handle the messages. In this outline, the fundamental structure of the Hut System was born.

Even though Welchman was a newcomer, both to codebreaking and to intelligence, the merits of his ideas were soon accepted. He later recalled: 'Travis' response was all I could have hoped for.... He quickly obtained official agreement to the establishment of a new section in the Bletchley Park complex to handle the possibility of Enigma breaks on an interservice basis.' In fact, it was not entirely inter-service: the navy wanted to be independent, and there were good reasons for this, since the naval version of Enigma used different 'indicators', and would be far more fiendish to break than 'ordinary' Army and Air Force Enigma. But the basics were accepted: Hut 6 would register the messages intercepted from army and air force sources, find the Enigma settings being used, and hand the results across to Hut 3, which would decipher, edit them ('emend', in Bletchley parlance, meaning to correct obvious typographical errors, fill in blanks where groups were garbled or omitted in transmission, and so forth), and turn them into intelligence. Similarly, on the naval side, Hut 8 would do registration and cryptanalysis, and Hut 4 would mirror the activity of Hut 3. Huts 3 and 6 were situated next to each other; the gap between them was sufficiently small that a wooden tunnel was constructed for communication between them. When papers needed to be sent from one hut to the other, they would be pushed through on a tray in the tunnel, using a string and broom handle for propulsion. The broom handle had a dual purpose: when a message was ready to be sent the handle was used to bang on the hatch as a signal. Such was the technology of Bletchley Park in the days of the huts.

Later in the war, the scale of activities and the number of personnel involved in each organization known as Hut 3, Hut 6, Hut 4 and Hut 8 outgrew the temporary wooden buildings hastily thrown up in the early months of the war. In fact, for most of 1941 and 1942 the eastern part of the site, between the old mansion house and the railway line, had become a building site. Large, unhandsome low-rise brick and concrete blocks sprang up. These may be ugly by modern standards but they were a substantial step-up in plushness and comfort for the staff who had endured the cold and dark of the huts. The organizations moved across to their new accommodation in 1942 and 1943, but kept their old designations: so Huts 3 and 6 were now in Block D, and their old wooden homes re-numbered. Along with the move came improvements in communications technology. Pressure-tube lines were installed along the building, with papers being rolled up and sent from one room to another at the speed of compressed air.

When it began, the Hut structure for Enigma codebreaking sat together with the pre-existing order of things at the GC&CS. At the outbreak of war, there had been three service sections, one for each

Women at work in 'Hut 6' after their move to Block D at Bletchley in 1943.

of the army, air force and navy, headed respectively by John Tiltman, Josh Cooper, and Frank Birch (see pages 16–17, Introduction). These were cryptography sections, reporting to their respective intelligence services: so, for example, Tiltman's section reported into the Director of Military Intelligence, his section being camouflaged with the name 'Number IV Intelligence School'. This arrangement naturally led to the heads of Huts 3 and 4 being service personnel – however, a move into intelligence was not always seen as a positive career step for a serving officer, as noted by Peter Calvocoressi when he joined up. Predictably enough, there were tensions, when the boffins and professors rubbed against the notional head of their section, who may (or may not) have been up to the job, but in any case was not skilled at handling the oddballs working under him.

John Tiltman (1894–1982)

John Tiltman ought to be known as the greatest cryptanalyst of the twentieth century. The list of his triumphs over impossible systems is enormously long. He broke codes and cipher systems of dozens of countries, in many cases involving languages he did not speak. He was Chief Cryptographer at Bletchley Park following Dilly Knox, and he was the only Bletchley codebreaker to reach the rank of Brigadier. He was made an OBE in 1930, a CBE in 1944 and a CMG in 1954. Yet outside specialist circles his name is hardly known, and that is a reflection of the secrecy which surrounded his art.

Tiltman showed his genius at an early age, being offered a place at Oxford University when only 13. But family circumstances prevented him accepting, and after a spell in teaching he joined the King's Own Scottish Borderers in

1914. As an officer in the trenches he was wounded and was decorated with the Military Cross. He stayed in the army after the war, and – in the climate of fear following the Bolshevik Revolution – in 1920 he attended a Russian language course. That opening saw him seconded to the fledgling GC&CS for a fortnight to translate a backlog of Russian decrypts. Tiltman never went back to regular army service.

He was posted to India, to France, to Hong Kong, to Finland and to the United States. Some of these missions were highly sensitive and all were deeply secret. He was instrumental in sorting out the diplomatic chaos which surrounded Alan Turing's liaison visit to America for the purpose of helping with American bombe machines. All the time he was in charge of the army section at Bletchley, and constantly unravelling new and complex codes.

Perhaps his greatest achievement was to assist the British with the development and implementation of new, secure, medium-grade ciphers to conceal the coded messages which had been read with success by German codebreakers. His 'stencil subtractor system' was quick and easy to use, while also baffling the Germans. This addition to security in British naval communications went a long way towards victory in the signals war in the Atlantic, and to overall victory over the U-boats.

Tiltman 'retired' from service with the British in 1954, but he continued as a consultant to both GCHQ and the NSA for another ten years. During this period he caught a bug, the desire to solve the mystery of the Voynich Manuscript – the one code (if indeed it is a code) to defeat John Tiltman.

The Voynich Manuscript is an extraordinary document held in the library at Yale University. It is named after the book dealer who purchased it in 1912, but it is much older, dating

John Tiltman, arguably Britain's greatest twentieth-century codebreaker.

from around 1420. It is heavily and exotically illustrated, with botanical drawings, astrological symbols and nude bathing ladies. But what makes it truly remarkable is the text. There is a lot of it, and it's in an unknown alphabet. Some say it's in code, others that it's in an unknown language, and about the only thing that everyone agrees on is that it is controversial. Every so often someone claims to have solved it, only to be knocked down by others.

Something like this is bound to attract the greatest cryptanalytic brains, even though Elizebeth Friedman, herself in the front rank of American codebreakers, said that attacks on the text were 'doomed to utter frustration'. As well as John Tiltman, fellow codebreakers William and Elizebeth Friedman, and Prescott Currier have tried their hand at deciphering it – all unsuccessfully. Nevertheless, the pictures are fun, even if you can't understand the captions.

J.E.S. (Josh) Cooper (1901–81)

When the public were first informed about the role, and significance, of the work done at Bletchley Park during World War II, very little technical information was made available. But what could be talked about were the people who worked there and their characteristics. One of the by-products of the drip-feed of knowledge was that the eccentricities and idiosyncrasies of the codebreakers attained a prominence which, given the breadth and depth of information now available, they might not have deserved.

One person whose achievements have been overshadowed by the notion that Bletchley Park was populated by eccentric boffins is J.E.S. (Josh) Cooper. At Bletchley Park, Cooper was well known for unconventional behaviour, such as throwing his coffee cup into the lake when it was empty. In his office there was a German air force map with the German grid references for the North Sea, recovered from a downed plane, complete with bloodstains. The map was called 'Lady Macbeth', because Cooper had tried to have it cleaned up, without success.

After studying languages at university, he joined Denniston's GC&CS in 1925 as a cryptanalyst. In 1936 he was seconded to the Air Ministry to analyse decrypted material, and from then he became GC&CS's air section head. Initially, GC&CS was expected to do no more than decryption, leaving all analysis to the service ministry: Cooper changed this and integrated interpretation with preparation of decrypts. After the war, he stayed at GCHQ until retirement, becoming head of research, a role to which he was better suited than administration. For his services, he became a CMG and a CB.

Unhappiness in Hut 3 was the source of one of the two uncomfortable reports reaching Alastair Denniston in the last part of 1941. Shortly after the Dunkirk debacle, a squadron leader was put in charge of Hut 3's air intelligence sub-group. His self-directed mission was to improve and standardize Hut 3's reporting and commentary, but he was in conflict with the actual head of Hut 3 for primacy in the Hut. It was not a happy time, with intelligence officers picking holes in the watchkeepers' work – watchkeepers being the wartime recruits without the training which regular-forces personnel might have. Likewise, the watchkeepers noted deficiencies in the performance of the trained officers, for example gaps

J.E.S. (Josh) Cooper, head of the Air Section at Bletchley Park.

in their knowledge about geography or language, where the outsiders had real expertise to offer. The system was broken.

But the system could be saved. Peter Calvocoressi recorded: 'Unified control was restored in 1942 in the shape of an officer from Air Ministry Intelligence who did not at first sight seem the right man for the job but emphatically was. He was unlike other senior people in the Hut, neither don nor schoolmaster, neither professional man nor intellectual. He came from the north Midlands where he was believed to have had something to do with biscuits.' The man from the north was Squadron Leader Eric Jones (see pages 223–4, Chapter 9), and he had nothing to do with biscuits. Instead, he stamped his calm and fair authority onto the Hut. He was such a success in this role that he didn't go back to industry after the war, but stayed on at GCHQ, eventually succeeding Sir Edward Travis as its head.

Not everyone in Hut 3 – or any hut, for that matter – had the exciting job of preparing intelligence or decoding the enemy's secret plans. Not only were a great deal of the deciphered messages extremely dull or technical, but there was a corresponding amount of filing, registration, typing and deciphering – which involved long hours at a typewriter-like device (British Typex machines converted to emulate Enigmas) hammering in gibberish to produce barely-recognizable German on long strips of ticker tape. All these tasks were vital, and most of them were dull to the point of distraction.

Drudgery, debs and dons

Many of the dull tasks were assigned to women clerical staff. A typical case was that of Jean Campbell-Harris, who joined Bletchley Park in 1942 aged only 18. Of her time in the naval section, where she sorted records, she said 'the job itself was deeply tedious: we were cipher clerks and we simply typed. We had to transcribe German naval code from a tape in five-letter groups, each one with a Z at the front, and it was extremely repetitive. Once we had finished transcribing the code, it was sent across the corridor to the team in the room opposite. I still don't really know what happened to the code once it got there. You didn't ask, you just did.' She also said that when they were off duty, she and her friends Osla Benning and Sarah (Sally) Norton would get the train to London, dance all night at the 400 Club in Leicester Square, and catch the milk train back to Bletchley in the morning. This was a typical experience among the famous group of 'debs', the upper-class female recruits who had joined Bletchley Park because they were connected to somebody, and owing to their social origins those in control assumed they could be trusted with secret work. There is also the tale of the laundry basket. 'Once, Osla and Sally bundled me into a large laundry basket on wheels that was used to move secret files and then pushed it down the corridor. It's not true, though it has been said, that I went careering into the gents' loo. In fact, I went straight into the office that was right at the end of the corridor. The occupant of the office, Geoffrey Tandy, had already decided that he did not like me and now he was absolutely furious.' High-jinks with laundry baskets were not the typical Bletchley experience, and in fact the number of debs at Bletchley was small, and their contribution equally so in comparison with the vast army of uncomplaining Wrens, ATS girls (army auxiliaries) and WAAFs (air force auxiliaries), who were also assigned tedious jobs.

Jean Campbell-Harris (Baroness Trumpington) (1922–2018)

Jean Campbell-Harris left school at 15, sent to study French and German abroad, and was only 17 when the war began. She started out on a fruit farm owned by the former prime minister David Lloyd George, which soon palled, but with her language skills and connections she was placed with the naval section at Bletchley typing up German naval signals. That job was boring too.

Bletchley Park famously recruited 'debs' as well as many young women from all walks of life; one of the debs was Osla Benning, shown here (left) in 1939.

But Jean Campbell-Harris was never herself boring. As a headmaster's wife in the 1950s she jumped into the swimming pool, fully dressed, on speech day; she famously gave the V-sign to Lord King in 2011 in the House of Lords when he remarked that the Bletchley Park veterans were getting old. She had a vibrant career as a Conservative in politics. 'I have met David Lloyd George, Max Beaverbrook, Jackie Kennedy, Bette Davis, Senator McCarthy, Stanley Spencer. Come to think of it, I have in fact met every single postwar prime minister, from Clement Attlee (who I met at the theatre) to David Cameron, and practically every world leader from Her Majesty the Queen to the Assads, Fidel Castro and Robert Mugabe.' She might have added that she met Alan Turing at Bletchley. Her final achievement, two days before she died, was to be invested in the Légion d'Honneur for her wartime service at Bletchley Park.

It is something of a myth, though, that all the women at Bletchley were debs or Wrens doing drudgery. Women may not have been recognized until recently as having roles equivalent to the men alongside whom they served, since in those days certain job types were classified as men's and others as women's. There were no codebreaker jobs for women, so women doing codebreaking were given inappropriate labels – women's job titles – such as 'translator' or 'clerical', which obscured the nature of the contribution they were actually making. Thus, the university girls typically had high-grade jobs, doing codebreaking in Huts 6 and 8, or in the diplomatic and commercial section; others had intelligence roles in Huts 3 and 4. For example, Winifred Evans, who came from Girton College, Cambridge, worked in the air section in Hut 6, and when it was set up she joined 'SIXTA', the sub-group of Hut 6 squeezing intelligence out of 'traffic analysis', the examination of what today would be called metadata in and around intercepted messages, whether or not they were actually deciphered.

Dealing with call signs and other message information, which wrapped the encoded content, was a non-trivial yet highly valuable occupation. For one thing, Bletchley Park depended to an extent on messages sent in one cipher, or one key, being forwarded on in another: breaking one message provided a way to strip off the cipher from the other. The traffic analysts were able to spot the cases where duplication occurred. Sometimes the senders of messages concealed their identity in the preamble, but the traffic analysts could build up a picture of who was involved by monitoring usage of radio frequencies and by other habits such as who would typically re-transmit messages.

Hut 4, and the rest of the naval section, boasted a range of talent of both sexes. In Hut 4, Walter Ettinghausen translated German Naval Enigma messages, which was more complicated than it sounds: the work involved disentangling corruptions in the text, interpreting abbreviations and jargon – and he knew that 'the life-and-death struggle against Germany's U-boats depended on the excellence of our product.' But the battle at sea was not just about breaking the U-boat codes. In particular, the war in the Mediterranean required the British to tackle the Italian naval messages, and this was work done outside Huts 4 and 8, which were after all the Enigma-focused division of Bletchley Park's naval section.

Walter Ettinghausen (Eytan) (1910–2001)

Walter Ettinghausen was born in Munich. During his childhood, his family moved to Britain, and he subsequently

Walter Ettinghausen, later Eytan, who became a senior figure in the Government of Israel after he left GC&CS.

became one of those 'men of the Professor type', lecturing in Medieval German at Oxford University. He was said to be 'fat, jolly and rather good-looking, but you didn't mess around with him' at Bletchley. After the war, he emigrated to Palestine, changing his name to Eytan, and when the State of Israel was established in 1948 he became the first director-general of its Foreign Ministry. He helped negotiate the peace settlement with Egypt after the first Arab-Israeli war and another with the Kingdom of Transjordan at the same time. During the 1950s he was an opponent of the tough retaliatory policy against Arab incursions, and during the next 20 years he continued to try to smooth the diplomatic relations between Israel and its neighbours. Given his background at Bletchley, it is not surprising to discover him involved in the establishment of Mossad.

Looking back on his time at Bletchley in 1993, Walter Eytan wrote: 'Our original family name was Ettinghausen, and we were born in Germany. The security clearance must have been singularly perceptive, since such antecedents might so easily have disqualified us.... I suppose the responsible officer, knowing or discerning that we were Jews, must have concluded, correctly, that we had an extra interest in fighting Hitler.... I may be the only one who will recall a peculiarly poignant moment when in late 1943 or early 1944 we intercepted a signal from a small German-commissioned vessel in the Aegean, reporting that it was transporting Jews, en route for Piraeus *zur Endlösung* ("for the final solution"). I had never seen or heard this expression before, but instinctively I knew what it must mean....'

Although the Italians had used Enigma, this was not the only cipher machine they relied on. Another rotor-based device was the C38M. This was a hand-cranked machine with no electrical components. Encipherment was done by a type of Caesar-shift: each letter would be transformed into another by adding a certain number to it, so if the number 5 was added to A it would become F. The number in question changed with each letter of the message, because of the action of the rotors in the machine, which had settable pins to change the cipher from one message to another. Bletchley Park's codebreakers were equal to the task, breaking the C38M and thereby allowing the British to interrupt the supply of shipping to Rommel in North Africa. When the fall of Mussolini's government came to pass in 1943, though, the codebreakers who had been working on Italian problems – including Madge Dale and Edward Simpson – needed a new role.

Madge Dale (1901–67)

Madge Dale has the distinction of being one of two women (among 73 names) on Alastair Denniston's March 1939 list of 'men of the Professor type' who might be called up for codebreaking duty in the event of war. She was a fellow of Lady Margaret Hall, Oxford, at the time, teaching classics there after having graduated in the same subject from the same university (but a different college), with a stint of school-teaching in between.

Bletchley was, for her, a period of 'conscription', and an unwelcome severance from LMH. About the work itself, of course, she did not speak. After her time there, where her most distinguished work was on Japanese telegrams, she went with her husband to the University of London, where she did become a professor, and renowned for a translation of Aeschylus' *Agamemnon*.

She was highly cultured, generous ('she spent a dauntingly high proportion of her income on keeping an ageing invalid connection in a nursing-home'), and suffered from appalling asthma (she weighed a mere 38 kg/84 lb at one point). Yet 'she was game for a show – it might be Gilbert and Sullivan or ballet or Pirandello – or she would discuss with wit and wisdom the latest Iris Murdoch novel, world politics, a Swedish yoghurt recipe or the *nouvelle critique* controversy.'[10]

Edward Simpson (1922–2019)

Edward Simpson was brought up in Northern Ireland. He read mathematics at Belfast, and joined Bletchley Park on graduation in 1942. He was put onto Italian machine ciphers, being one of the team who broke the Hagelin C38M machine used by the Italian Navy. Later he went on to break Japanese traffic.

After the war, Simpson went to take a PhD at Cambridge University, where in 1951 he described a statistical phenomenon which can happen when two groups of data are combined. Although each group, on its own, implies a trend in one direction, the combined set may imply the opposite. The phenomenon is now known as Simpson's paradox. His insight,

10 Obituary in the 'Brown Book', published by Lady Margaret Hall.

in some degree, had its foundation in the interpretation of data which went on at Bletchley Park.

Simpson's career was in the Civil Service, including a stint working for Lord Hailsham, and eventually rising to be Deputy Secretary at the Department of Education and Science. He remained an energetic supporter of Bletchley Park, serving on the modern museum's Historical Advisory Group until his death in 2019.

Looking east

Although Italy was out of the war as an enemy, since December 1941 there had been a new one in the shape of Japan. The received wisdom was that it was impossible for British people, even linguists, to master Japanese in less than two years, so work against Japanese codes and ciphers had been rather neglected. But John Tiltman knew better. He had successfully tackled a range of different Japanese ciphers during the 1930s, and recognized that a comprehensive understanding of the Japanese language was not what was required to be a successful codebreaker. Moreover, he was a teacher. The cover name 'Number IV Intelligence School' was, in part, not cover at all, since in the gas showrooms at Bedford the School was teaching people the rudiments of codes and ciphers and codebreaking. So Tiltman instigated a crash course in Japanese for the redundant Italian section, which could be completed in six months.

Before 1943 only a handful of codebreakers, principally Tiltman himself, had focused on Japanese material. But once Japan had become a belligerent, this needed to change, and the Japanese section at Bletchley expanded from a corner of Hut 10 into the space in Hut 4 previously occupied with Italian naval messages. Alexis Vlasto, one of the dons from King's College, Cambridge, came to head up the section tackling the Japanese Army Air Force's General Purpose Code. It was a book code, needing to be painstakingly rebuilt, Room 40 fashion, with the aid of meticulously recorded data held in a special index. This kind of job did not need detailed knowledge of Japanese, but a head for organization and detail. And, ideally, good chess or table tennis skills, since the Japanese section codebreakers were fond of those spare time activities.

Chess has often been thought of as a defining characteristic of Bletchley Park's codebreakers, though in fact some of them, like Alan Turing and Donald Michie (see pages 225–7, Chapter 9), were not in the league of super-players (and had to play each other if they were going to have a tolerable game). The super-players were there, though, in abundance, including Hugh Alexander and Stuart Milner-Barry (see pages 110–11, Chapter 4); Harry Golombek, like Alexander, was a member of the British chess team; James Macrae Aitken, the Scottish champion was there; and I.J. Good (see pages 225–7, Chapter 9) was the champion of Cambridge University. Golombek and Alexander would hold evenings when they would take on 20 other codebreakers at once, walking round the room from board to board. Naturally enough, the codebreakers formed their own chess team, which took on Oxford University in a match in December 1944. The mind boggles about the secrecy implications, with a team from an obscure place called Bletchley beating Oxford 8-4, especially as the match was reported in *Chess* magazine in February 1945.

Back at work, there was a war to win. The war in Europe always loomed larger in the British consciousness, but Japanese coded messages were highly important, and not just for the war in the far east. They gave the British not just tactically useful information like convoy movements, but also what was being planned between Japan and her Germany ally. The intelligence included details of shipments of pitchblende – uranium ore – being sent to Japan by U-boat under cover of a delivery of lead, possibly as a protection from the radioactivity. But perhaps the most significant set of Japanese messages

Harry Golombek (left) would take on 20 codebreakers at once in a Bletchley Park chess marathon.

came from the Japanese embassy in Berlin, where Baron Oshima, the ambassador, had frequent and detailed conversations with Adolf Hitler himself. His reports back to Tokyo gave the fullest details, from 1941 onwards, of German thinking at the highest level, and they showed (among other things) how the Germans had swallowed the deception plans masking the true place for the invasion of France in 1944.

The U-boat war

Back in 1943, the situation in Italy may have signalled a turning point in the war for the Allies, but in part the turnaround was due to a resolution of see-sawing fortunes in the North Atlantic. Since the earliest days at Bletchley Park, the naval version of Enigma was the biggest challenge, and as Britain's dependency on convoys grew, the importance of solving the problem increased in importance.

To begin with, the German Navy used a different 'indicator' system from that in use in their air force and army to tell the message recipient how to set up his Enigma machine. Where the army and air force told the operator to choose a random sequence of three letters and set the rotors at these, the navy had a rulebook requiring the choice to be made according to a complex set of principles, and then encoded using 'bigram tables' before sending. Although Alan Turing had unravelled the principles of the system as early as 1939, and developed a technique called 'Banburismus' for finding the right-most rotor being used, this didn't help as much as one might think. There were two ways to find out the Enigma settings being used: to test an intercept against a 'crib', using a bombe, or to use Banburismus. But cribs did not grow on trees: to guess at the content of Naval Enigma messages, one needed to have broken some messages first. So that was no good. But to use Banburismus, you needed to have the bigram tables...

With blessed good fortune, in early 1940 a German vessel was captured together with its secret books, including the all-important bigram tables. Banburismus was an intellectual challenge, but one that was addictive, as Joan Clarke recorded in 1993: 'Rolf Noskwith reminded me that Banburismus was often so enthralling that the analyst due to go home at the end of the shift would be unwilling to hand over the workings: he was too polite to say that I had been a particular culprit.' As well as Banburismus, there was 'Yoxallismus', a statistical method invented by codebreaker Leslie Yoxall for finding cross-pluggings on special German messages marked for decryption by officers only. Joan Clarke also noted wryly, 'My own contribution, a day or two later, greatly speeded up the routine solutions, but my name was not attached to it: I was told, to my surprise, that I had used "pure Dillyismus".' At this time, Joan and Alan Turing became very close, and the short and unhappy story of their engagement followed.

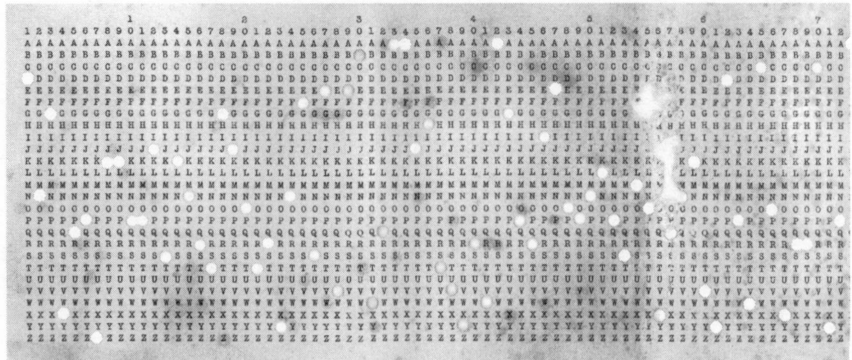

'Banbury sheets' were printed at Banbury and used by codebreakers to help identify the right-most rotor of the German naval Enigma machine.

Joan Clarke (1917–96)

When Gordon Welchman approached Joan Clarke, one of his brightest mathematics students at Cambridge, about joining Bletchley Park, 'he said that the work did not really need mathematics but mathematicians tended to be good at it.'[11] That was enough to attract her, without her having the faintest idea what the work would actually involve. She was so good at it, in fact, that there was a problem: how to promote her, given that she was doing a cryptanalyst's job, but that promotion onto the cryptanalyst career ladder was forbidden by the gender-orientated rules in force in 1940. The answer was that she became a linguist. She duly filled in the form ('Grade applied for: Linguist. Language skills: None.') and got the promotion. By the end of World War II Joan Clarke was deputy head of Hut 8.

---

11 Joan Clarke (as Joan Murray) in Hinsley and Stripp (eds.), *Codebreakers: The Inside Story of Bletchley Park* (2001), chapter 14.

She got on famously with Alan Turing, who for probably the first time in his life had met a girl who shared his interests. They were forever in each other's company and everyone thought them well-suited. They became engaged, and then Turing dropped the bombshell – he had 'homosexual tendencies'. After some pause for thought, the engagement was off, though the friendship stayed in place.

Joan Clarke transferred to GCHQ after the war ended, where she met her husband. During a spell away from GCHQ she became interested in numismatic history, contributing an important study on Scottish coins of the sixteenth and seventeenth centuries. This work was, in fact, a species of codebreaking, since the puzzle of what sequence the coins had followed had defeated scholars in the past. In 1962 she went back to GCHQ, where she stayed working on secret problems until her retirement in 1977. At that time the Enigma story was just breaking into the public domain, and her post-retirement roles included helping F.H. Hinsley with the multi-volume history, *British Intelligence in the Second World War*. She was a private person, liked and admired by her colleagues, and an outstanding example of someone who, in a modest and understated way, broke through the gender ceiling of her age.

Other relationships were more securely founded, though in the beginning mixed-gender working was an innovation. The principal problem was not mixing men and women together, but the shift system. When this was introduced into Hut 6 in 1940, it was thought necessary to have a minimum of six 'girls' in the Hut during the night shift, owing to the moral danger. The Hut had a complement of three available, which was thought 'insufficient to ensure the observance of the proprieties',

Joan Clarke at the time of her wedding, after the war.

so three extra women were drafted in from the team using punched cardboard sheets to break Enigma (this was the time before the bombes became operational). The three extras had nothing to do, and their role as chaperones was soon discontinued. In due time, maybe because of the absence of the chaperones, a whole host of relationships sprang up, and many marriages resulted. Of those we have encountered before, Madge Dale met her husband Professor Tom Webster (omitted, for some reason, from Alastair Denniston's list of 'professors') at Bletchley; Mavis Lever met her husband Keith Batey there; and Edward Simpson met his wife Rebecca Gibson when he was sent to meet her, as a fellow graduate of Queen's University Belfast, at the station on her first day at Bletchley.

Another relationship forged at Bletchley in the naval section involved Patrick Wilkinson from King's College, Cambridge.

> *In January 1942 a girl called Sydney Eason arrived in our Subsection, aged nearly 18. She had been recruited in the normal BP kind of way: a friend of her family who lived near where W.F. Clarke was billeted wrote to say that there was an institution near there which seemed to employ girls for war work with no qualifications. At 6 ft 2 ins., she was half an inch taller than I was. Indeed, we first became conscious of one another because, working on opposite sides of a very wide table, we kept having to apologise for accidentally kicking each other.*

Of such stuff romances are made. Patrick and Sydney were married on 16 February 1944, and then it was back to Bletchley Park where, now there was no need for work on Italian naval codes, Patrick was put in the Hut 3 research section under his fellow Kingsman Peter Lucas.

While Patrick and Sydney had been beginning their under-the-table *pas de deux* in the naval section, those working on Naval Enigma were having a tough time of it. There were several differences between the German Naval Enigma and the other armed forces. One was that the navy had three extra rotors at their disposal for each Enigma machine, making a total of eight. The extra three rotors had different wiring, but identical turnover notch-positions, which made the job of the 'Banburists' particularly hard. Nonetheless, 1941 was described by Joan Clarke as the heyday of Banburismus. During that year, the British were able to identify the probable attack plans of the U-boats, and re-route many convoys away from danger. But changes were afoot in the German Naval High Command. A new Enigma machine, using four rotors instead of three, was going to come into use. At a stroke, Banburismus would be rendered impossible, and the bombe machines almost redundant, since 26 machines would be needed to test a single crib if they were to cope with the extra permutations implied with a fourth rotor.

Initially, Bletchley Park had no answer to the four-rotor Enigma problem. It would take new feats of engineering, and more fraught disagreements, to get on top of that. 1942 was going to be a difficult year for the convoys; it was even worse than Bletchley Park being locked out of the secret German U-boat signals, though, because the German naval codebreaking service was reading the British codes and so knew exactly where the convoys were going to be. Once again, the sinkings of merchant ships were rising, this time to unprecedented levels. If the war was to be won, the convoys had to get through. Solving the four-rotor problem was, literally, a matter of life or death. But the British had a secret weapon. They were now in full partnership with America, and American codebreakers would play a vital role in the battle of the Atlantic.

CHAPTER 7
The Americans

In the dark days for Britain, back in 1940 after France had agreed an Armistice with Germany, Winston Churchill had just one simple priority for the country. To save Britain, it was essential to bring America into the war, formally or informally. No effort was spared to achieve that result. Over the coming months, arrangements of all kinds, most of them entirely without precedent, were brought into being: Lend-Lease, the destroyers-for-bases deal, convoy escorting – and intelligence sharing.

None of this was straightforward, particularly in 1940 when Roosevelt faced a presidential election in which the most visibly pacifist candidate was assured victory, and the wise voices from London knew it was just a matter of time before the lah-di-dah Empire diehards capitulated along with their nineteenth-century attitudes. Fortunately, the personal relationship between Churchill and Roosevelt was secure enough to allow some facts to intrude, beginning with a visit to Washington by Sir Henry Tizard, chairman of the Aeronautical Research Committee, in September 1940, where Britain would show America its most up-to-date and exciting technological innovations. In a sense, it was a replay of what the Poles had tried the year before, to draw the Americans into closer military cooperation and planning, by revealing the secrets which could only be exploited through a full partnership.

There was little to lose for America, just to listen to what the British delegation had to say about radar, proximity fuses, jet engines and 'tube alloys' (the cover name for a potential atomic bomb). There was also a host of other gadgets, ideas and weaponry. And there was the hint of something more, something abstract – something to do with codebreaking. It's not clear from whom the directive came, but William F. Friedman, the US Army's chief cryptanalyst, was instructed to put together a proposal for exchange of cryptanalytic secrets.

Clearly such a proposal was absurd. Where would it end? What if the British were trying to break American messages? America's principal threat came from Japan, not Germany, and the value of such an exchange was questionable. The biggest doubt was whether either side could trust the other to keep the top secrets top secret. But the British might have some technical ideas, thoughts about techniques, which could be useful. The proposal gained the support of Brigadier General George V. Strong, head of US Army intelligence, and Brigadier General Joseph O. Mauborgne, head of the US Signal Corps (who had been suitably impressed by the British demonstrations of radar and identification-of-friend-or-foe technologies during the Tizard meetings). Except that the US Navy was not yet on board, it might actually happen. But Roosevelt had been Secretary of the Navy before he became President, and a political approach to his successor as Secretary brought them around. The Americans were going to share cryptanalytic work.

Trial by sherry

It was perhaps a shame that nobody had checked with the GC&CS whether this suited them. Initially, the answer was 'No': the publication in 1931 by the American cryptanalyst Herbert O. Yardley of an exposé of American codebreaking and spying during and after World War I meant that the security question was bound to be there. America was not in the war; Italians and Germans might get access to the secrets, and lock Britain out of the ciphers so painfully won.

Again, the politicians' vision brought about the impossible. Just after Christmas 1940, William Friedman was ordered to travel to Britain. Illness prevented him going, but by mid-January a replacement team had been selected. Representing the US would be Captain

Abraham Sinkov for the Army and Lieutenant Prescott Currier for the navy, together with Lieutenant Leo Rosen and Ensign Robert Weeks as technical experts. They sailed on HMS *King George V* on 25 January 1941, whose duty was to escort a convoy of merchantmen crossing the Atlantic at 11 knots. The convoy's most precious cargo was a secret box, stowed somewhere in the bowels of the battleship. The name of the cargo was 'Purple'. And the journey was precarious. Prescott Currier wrote:

> *We were going down the swept channel on the east coast of England where all of the convoys traveled. The following noon we approached a convoy ... a reconnaissance bomber came overhead and saw the convoy and saw us and we all knew what this meant ... we all went below decks and sat there. I was trying to eat some soup but my mouth was so dry I couldn't swallow it. I've never been so scared in my life. We heard a bomb landing on one side and one on the other side and the ship would bounce out of the water and back down again. The I heard something that sounded like someone dragging chains along the deck. The Germans were making strafing runs...*

On arrival, in their civilian clothes, into a cold war-torn country, the four junior American officers must have experienced some degree of cultural dislocation. The British greeting at Bletchley Park was a bizarre ritual of gothic proportions, according to Currier:

> *The countryside was pitch black with rarely a light showing except for the faint glow emanating from a small hole scraped in the blacked-out headlight lens of the cars. When we arrived at BP, the large brick mansion was barely visible; not a glimmer of light showed through the blackout curtains. We were led through the main doors, and after passing through a blacked-out vestibule, into a dimly lit hallway, then into the office of Commander Denniston.*

The ordeal had barely begun. Denniston's personal assistant, Barbara Abernethy, picks up the story: 'Denniston rang the bell and I struggled in [with a great big cask from the Army & Navy Stores] and somehow managed to pour glasses of sherry for these poor Americans, who I kept looking at. I'd never seen Americans before, except in the films. I just plied them with sherry.'

The 'poor Americans' were at Bletchley for a month or so.

Abraham Sinkov (1907–98)
Prescott H. Currier (1912–95)

Abraham Sinkov took the US Civil Service examination in 1930. His skills in mathematics and languages led to him being offered a post in cryptanalysis – a subject about which he knew nothing. That had changed by 1941 when he was sent on the secret mission to the UK to liaise with Bletchley Park. He may have been chosen for his diplomatic and organizational perception; later in the war, when tensions over ownership of codebreaking capabilities against Japan threatened the harmony between US and Australian codebreaking teams, it was Sinkov, now based in Melbourne, that re-established harmony and brought valuable signals intelligence to General Douglas MacArthur.

Prescott Currier enlisted in the US Navy, attending college after discharge, but then finding himself with a Civil Service post in Op-20-G, using his language and analytical skills in the navy's codebreaking service. After World War II he held a variety of intelligence jobs, including two stints as liaison officer between the US and the UK, one at GCHQ and another at diplomatic level. In retirement, Currier's analysis of

Abraham Sinkov, leader of the secret American mission to Bletchley Park in 1941.

the statistical patterns of the Voynich manuscript led him to conclude that two different languages were used by its writer; the mysterious manuscript remains unsolved.

During their visit the Americans were shown a wealth of treasures: the Enigma, Hollerith punched-card machinery used for preparing difference tables in stripping off super-encipherments, German, Italian and Russian codes, intercept stations, and the processing of signals into intelligence. The Brits thought they were doing their bit. On their side, the Americans handed over their special, priceless gift. This thing, called Purple, was not purple at all; and it was a huge, heavy reconstruction of a Japanese encipherment machine. It was a triumph of cryptanalysis. William Friedman, together with Leo Rosen – one of the four 'poor Americans' visiting Bletchley – had reverse-engineered the Japanese machine through pure cryptanalysis. It was a feat matching that of Marian Rejewski with the Enigma, and the Americans were giving the British one of their rare examples of their rebuilt machine which emulated exactly the behaviour of the Japanese device, which none of them had ever seen.

And this is where the trouble began. In return, the Americans were expecting to receive, at least, an Enigma machine. But the British had no Enigma machines to spare. There was no lack of sharing: the British willingly handed over a 'paper' version of an Enigma, which is to say the drawings. But the British were still steeped in nervousness about security, so the expression of willingness took the form of further ritual: a solemn written undertaking, signed by Sinkov, to disclose nothing about the attack on Enigma, except 'by word of mouth' to Commander Laurence F. Safford, USN, his commanding officer. And it had taken four weeks to get to this stage, the point where the British could show the Americans the biggest secret on their side – the secret of the bombe.

Meanwhile, the four American visitors had been royally looked after. They were put up in a manor house, and experienced 'really elegant living', spared the brutality of rationing because the manor had a working farm with plentiful fresh produce. They had a car and were able to visit the Cotswolds and other places as well as learn about British cryptanalysis. On one such trip, Currier recalled:

> *Our driver was a Scottie with a very strong Highland accent and none of the English could understand it. We ... were stopped at a road block by local police. This was done all over England. And there they had a [military] vehicle with two men in civilian clothes in the back seat, obviously not British, a Scottish driver that they couldn't understand, and he got out there and stamped his feet... 'See, ya conno do this, they're on a secret mission.'*

They got arrested anyway, but were soon released. At Bletchley Park, the four thought they were being shown everything: they 'were permitted to come and go freely and to visit and talk with anyone in any area that interested us,' and they came to understand the working conditions: 'Furnishings were sparse: a desk with a chair for each of us, a pad of paper and few pencils. The rooms were a bit cold and uncarpeted and a bit dusty but we soon found out that this was a condition common to all work spaces, including the Director's.' The machinations of what could and what could not be disclosed were going on without their knowledge, and by the end of their visit it seemed that all had come out right in the end.

Almost: there were still some hiccups. Commander Safford had opposed the cryptanalytical sharing from the outset, and consistently with Sinkov's undertaking the formal written report of the visit made no mention of the Enigma disclosures. Worse, there was a muddle over the 'paper Enigma', which could not be properly understood since one of the documents went astray in Washington. Worse still, there was a misunderstanding between the two US service departments: the army had a commercial Enigma machine, while the navy did not, and so technical issues which were obvious to the army were a source of puzzlement to the navy, who thought they were being deliberately kept from vital information. With nothing of substance about Enigma in the report, no machine, an incomplete set of papers, and muddle all round it was only too easy to accuse the British of bad faith and incomplete disclosure and demonstrate that the whole thing had been a waste of time. It would take much more hard work on both sides before cryptanalytical sharing matured into a real partnership. More than that, it would take the transformation of a European conflict into a world war.

BRUSA

The first indications were given in the spring of 1941; by the autumn it was a certainty. The Germans were going to change the Enigma machine which they were using to direct U-boats in the battle with the convoys in the Atlantic Ocean. The new version was going to have a fourth rotor, which, at a stroke, would render the three-rotor bombes which had been helping with convoy routing during the second half of that year. The fatal day was 1 February 1942: Britain was locked out of what Bletchley Park called 'Shark', the four-rotor Enigma cipher.

For Americans, the idea that the introduction of Shark was of life-threatening proportions must have seemed like an absurd exaggeration. The attack on Pearl Harbor in December 1941 had dragged America into the war, and it was apparent to all that the threat to America came from Japan. Yet Adolf Hitler had made the mistake of declaring war on America shortly after the attack, and that made American shipping fair game for the U-boats.

During the first few months of 1942, before the US Navy introduced mandatory convoying along the American east coast, the U-boats had what their captains called the 'happy time': lying in wait for the unescorted ships to steam along the north-south route, beautifully silhouetted against the brightly-lit towns of the eastern seaboard. Picking off the targets could not have been simpler. The sinkings rose and the U-boat captains won decorations. All at the time when the British could produce nothing of any value from Enigma decrypts, which were closed-off owing to the introduction of Shark.

Something needed to be done, and it needed to be done quickly.

The climate for international cooperation was still chilly after the mistrust and half-done sharing attempt of 1941. The American naval codebreaking unit in Washington, called Op-20-G, had its hands full with the Japanese problem, with the result that its efforts to adapt what they had learned about Enigma and bombes in 1941 to the new challenge in the Atlantic was falling behind. The obvious answer was a division of labour: the British to work on Enigma and the Americans to focus on Japan. Fresh overtures were made; John Tiltman (see pages 133–7, Chapter 6) visited Op-20-G in April, and dialogue between Op-20-G and Commander Edward Travis (see pages 123–5, Chapter 5), now in charge at Bletchley, continued with updates on progress against the four-rotor problem.

In fact, progress was slow; too slow for the Americans. It may be that Britain was going to get on top of the four-rotor problem eventually, but countless ships would be sunk and lives lost if the issue was not tackled more aggressively and with new technology. The Americans decided to initiate their own project to design and build a new kind of bombe that could kill the Shark.

Travis accepted the reality of this situation, while also offering a British machine when it was ready, and inviting a further mission of American codebreakers 'to find out all details possible concerning the British "E" problem.' So it was that US Navy lieutenants (junior grade) Robert B. Ely and Joseph J. Eachus made the transatlantic crossing to be inducted into the mysteries of Bletchley Park. The staff at Bletchley Park had all signed a copy of the Official Secrets Act, an initiation ritual which was part of the mystery – and that meant that no disclosures were going to be made to a visiting American, at least not without some unusual arrangements. Those arrangements were duly made – and they included the supply of sugar. Joseph Eachus found himself designated by the US Navy as a 'detached unit', which meant that he could draw supplies just like other detached units, which typically referred to entire ships. So, he was able to get hold of sugar, in rationed Britain, in 100 lb (45 kg) sacks and coffee in 20 lb (9 kg) cans. 'Consequently, when I would go to some other office to ask them to tell me about what I was doing, I would take a cup of sugar with me, which made me a good deal more welcome than I might otherwise have been.' Eachus was being too modest. No doubt the sugar helped, but his own charm and intellectual contribution – including to the continually evolving bombe design – helped just as much.

Travis was building an understanding with his opposite numbers in Op-20-G, which culminated in a formal agreement, signed on 1 October 1942. For the first time, this set out the cooperation arrangements. The Americans were going to have first call on Japanese traffic – which meant that the British would have to disband their listening stations in Kenya and Australia, and rely on the Americans to pass on what they had decoded. (Meanwhile, the British could 'maintain a research unit at GC&CS so as not to lose touch with the Japanese problem'.) As to German signals, the British agreed to 'full collaboration upon the German submarine and naval cryptanalysis problems.' It was a bit lopsided: the British were giving up their predominance in codebreaking, as part of the price of closer working, though it was accepted on both sides that the British 'will be the coordinating head in the Atlantic theatre as the US will be in the Pacific'.[12] Demarcation of responsibility for attacks on Japanese codes was not easily agreed to – the Americans wanted exclusivity, but the British could not accept that they would be takers of whatever limited information they might be fed by their ally. Despite all these difficulties, present and future, the 1942 deal was a remarkable achievement. To share secrets, and to agree formally to do so, was a huge leap of faith for both countries. And the faith was kept. Travis' agreement of 1942 was to be the first

12 National Archives of the United Kingdom.

of a number of agreements, subsequently called 'BRUSA', standing for Britain-USA.

The Desch bombe

Meanwhile the Americans had not been waiting around for the British to sort out their problems developing a bombe capable of breaking four-rotor Enigma. In Dayton, Ohio, at the National Cash Register Corporation's factory, research was going on to develop a wholly new type of bombe. The project was led by Dr Joseph R. Desch, who had to solve the problem of getting the banks of drums (the rotating components of bombes which mimicked the action of the Enigma rotors) fast enough. The challenge was that a four-rotor Enigma has 456,976 possible rotor configurations. If ten configurations were tested every second, it would still take 12 hours to complete a test. The three-rotor bombes at Bletchley were able to do their job in just over ten minutes, which was realistic for same-day codebreaking; but 12 hours was not, for the machine settings would change every midnight.

Joseph R. Desch (1907–87)

Joe Desch was born in Dayton, Ohio, about a mile from the bicycle shop owned by the Wright Brothers. Engineering was in the air. Desch himself was already building a reputation as an innovative engineer when he joined the National Cash Register Corporation in 1938. One of his achievements was to build a digital electronic calculator – in 1940, when calculating machinery was still mechanical or relying on electrical relays, like the British bombe. But it was Desch's insight into the use of electronic valves or tubes for counting that led to his development of the American bombe.

Joe Desch, inventor of the partly-electronic American four-rotor bombe devised to attack U-boat Enigma.

The trouble was that developing the bombe was not a stress-free job, Desch had to act as host to permanent official guests, and his house was itself labelled a 'secure facility'. There was a navy guard who followed Desch around 24 hours a day. In November 1944, he walked out: 'They pushed me and pushed me and pushed me, and told me I had to get all this stuff done because our guys were dying.' Desch was not the only one to have been driven beyond the limit – the head of Op-20-G already reported one suicide and two breakdowns as early as 1940. Desch was coaxed back to work, but it was never going to be an easy relationship with his naval employers.

After the war, Desch developed the first completely solid-state computer, and served as a member of the NSA's Scientific Advisory Board.

In 1947, in a secret ceremony, Joe Desch received America's highest honour for civilian service, the National Medal of Merit. Only, because it was for secret work, he could not even tell his family why it had been awarded.

Joe Desch looked at the problem in another way. The real issue was not that the drums rotated too slowly – he could easily make them spin fast enough – the problem was 'overshoot'. When a Bletchley bombe had found a plausible Enigma setting, it would stop and then the operator could read out the rotor configuration from 'indicator' drums. But the sheer momentum of the rapidly spinning four-rotor machine drums would carry them far beyond the relevant point before they were able to stop.

Joe Desch was an electronics expert. He had been developing 'thyratron tubes' – gas-filled devices like light bulbs, which could operate as electronic switches – as counters. The tubes could be adapted to serve as a memory for the overshot stop position on his fast-moving bombes. Electronics had met the bombe.

One outcome of the BRUSA agreement brokered by Travis was that Alan Turing would make a visit to the United States. He had been there before – for two years, to study at Princeton University, returning in the autumn of 1938 when it had become clear that Britain was going to be embroiled in another war. This new visit had multiple purposes, all different from academic study. On the to-do list was to visit Desch in Dayton and discuss the development of the electronic bombe.

After a long train ride from the east coast, Alan Turing reached Dayton on 21 December 1942. He was accompanied by a number of US naval staff, Major Stevens of the British military liaison team in Washington, and Joseph Eachus whom Turing had met earlier in the year during Eachus' fact-finding visit to Bletchley. At the time, Desch's electronic memory mechanism was not yet developed, and overshoot was being tackled by rewinding the machine – which Turing thought unnecessary and likely to stress the machine. But other innovations were rather attractive: the use of switches rather than skeins of wire attached to physical jacks, which had to be manhandled every time the bombe was reprogrammed, and the 'resistor board' – a device to test several Enigma plug-board settings automatically, and Eachus' own innovation, thought up during his time at Bletchley – was being incorporated.

The trouble with Dr Turing

So, the American bombe project looked in fair order, though it would take a few more months to perfect the partly electronic design, and to sort out the manufacturing and other teething problems. The more immediate problem for Alan Turing was that there was nowhere to stay, so he ended up on a mattress in Joe Desch's house. One can speculate about the potential for discussions about electronics and computing machinery, and the influence on postwar computer development which may have taken place during Turing's handful of days in Dayton.

There were other purposes to his long stay in America in 1942–3. The visit to Dayton was just part: in Washington and New York there were other things to inspect and other people to see. Among these secret projects (so secret that, later, Turing had to deny to his friends that he had even visited America during the war) was the apparatus being developed under project code number X61753. The apparatus was huge. It used 40 racks for equipment and weighed 50 tons – and it was an attachment to a telephone line.

The secret project which Turing was sent to inspect was intended to solve the security problem inherent in Churchill's need to use the phone to speak to President Roosevelt. The physical telephone lines could be tapped, but security arrangements at both ends reduced the likelihood of that. The problem arose in the middle: across the Atlantic, the phone calls were being transmitted over wireless. If the wireless signals were not encrypted in some way they could be intercepted and anyone could listen in. And the Germans had been listening in. The huge X61753 apparatus, which would have to be installed at each end of the line, would encipher and decipher the conversation in real time, so that Churchill could deploy all his rhetorical powers on the patient president without Adolf Hitler finding out what he was saying.

All that was a fine plan, except that the BRUSA agreement was with the US Navy, not the US Army, and the US Army had no idea who Turing was, who he worked for, and how on earth anyone should imagine that this British person without valid US security clearance should be allowed to wander around their most secret facility.

The army's stance might have seemed like a comedy, but it nearly turned to tragedy. The British, obviously, wanted the new phone system to be checked out by their cryptological expert, so asked for the security clearance to be granted. The answer was 'No'. The problem was escalated, and the answer was still 'No'. The British then threatened to withdraw from the intelligence cooperation agreement so painfully stitched together over the previous two years – and Chief of Staff General George C. Marshall ordered that Turing could inspect the machine. Diplomatic disaster was averted, Alan Turing signed off on the apparatus, and in a few months a 'Sigsaly' machine was installed in London so that Churchill and Roosevelt could chat in safety.

Shipment 0192-A

While the fuss about the telephone encipherment was at full volume, the United States Army had more pressing concerns. In fact, it is astonishing that the X61753 business even reached Marshall's desk at this time – an indication of how seriously both sides were taking it. For the Americans had invaded North Africa in early November 1942, the second arm of a giant pincer intended to squash the life out of the *Deutsche Afrika Korps* and the joint German-Italian operation along the southern Mediterranean. The landings had gone well, but as the winter of 1942–3 settled around the American troops there had been some setbacks. The most substantial took place in February 1943, when the Americans were surprised and suffered heavily at the Battle of Kasserine Pass. The root cause was an intelligence failure. The liaison systems for getting Ultra – the 'special intelligence' derived from broken codes – were not working.

The need for an army version of the Travis BRUSA agreement was clear, particularly if it was Bletchley Park that was producing the decrypts and intelligence appreciations. On 17 May 1943, the United States War Department signed a new agreement with GC&CS. It was much bolder than the 1942 one: 'Both the US and British agree to exchange completely all information concerning the detection, identification and interception of signals from, and the solution of codes and ciphers used by, the Military and Air Forces of the Axis powers, including secret services (Abwehr).' And that was just clause 1. Signals intelligence cooperation had come of age.

A few weeks later, a new detachment of Americans assembled at Arlington Hall, a former girls' school just outside the centre of Washington, DC. Arlington Hall had become the headquarters of army and diplomatic codebreaking in America, a counterpart to the US Naval

Communications Annex, which was housed in the Mount Vernon College for Women (another former girls' school on the opposite side of the city). The recruits at Arlington found themselves designated as shipment number 0192-A, and their destination was Britain. They were led by William P. Bundy, 'no career signal intelligence person, having entered the army as a draftee in 1941, his demonstrated ability and his quietly effective personality, with its touch of Bostonian starch, were obvious qualifications for the job.'[13]

William P. Bundy (1917–2000)

Coming from a family of intellectuals it was probably inevitable that Bill Bundy would graduate top of his senior school class, then go on to read history at Yale, followed by Harvard and then Harvard Law School. War interrupted his design to go into the legal profession, and a posting to the US Army Signal Corps led to his work at Bletchley Park. When he left Britain, he had collected the US Legion of Merit honour and been awarded the OBE.

This, though, was the beginning. After a stint in a law firm, Bundy joined the CIA, moving into government as Assistant Secretary of State for Far Eastern Affairs and found himself in the unenviable position of advising on the Vietnam War. All three of Presidents Kennedy, Johnson and Nixon were counselled by Bundy on the strategy and the conflict. Bundy was critical of Henry Kissinger, Nixon's National Security Adviser, but Kissinger paid him a somewhat barbed tribute: 'Everyone in the State Department is trying to knife me in the

13 Thomas Parrish, *The Ultra Americans* (1986), p. 100.

back, except for Bill Bundy,' he complained, 'He is still enough of a gentleman to knife me in the chest.'

On leaving politics, Bundy became a professor at Princeton University. With such a remarkable CV, it may be surprising to read that Bundy described his time in Hut 3 as 'the most satisfying of my career'.

William P. Bundy became adviser to Presidents Kennedy, Johnson and Nixon on Vietnam after his time at Bletchley Park.

Passage across the Atlantic on the liner *Aquitania* for these proto-codebreakers was a mixture of comfort and endurance test. As officers, they were 'sat at tables with white table-cloths and were waited on by Cunard waiters.'[14] But the fare was unremittingly British: one of Bundy's companions, Selmer S. Norland, found kippers and kidneys hard to stomach at breakfast. On arrival in London, the Americans observed with amazement the devastation in the centre, with the stalwart cathedral of St Paul's somehow still standing amongst the rubble. There was beer, and there were girls, and there were trips to the theatre, so it was not all bad. At the end of August, they were sent to a nondescript place in the middle of nowhere: billeted in Bedford, some 32 km (20 miles) from Bletchley, and they commuted by train like regular office workers. Bundy himself was billeted in Leighton Buzzard, about 16 km (10 miles) from Bletchley but in the opposite direction, and his journey was by bus. Yet they were still a team, and they now had their own regimental number, the 6813th Signal Service Detachment.

Selmer S. Norland (1916–2016)

Selmer Norland was born on a farm in Iowa into a Norwegian-speaking family. On his first day at school, he told the teacher that she would have to learn Norwegian because he did not speak English. In time, Norland became a superb linguist, taking German as part of his degree and then going on to teach the subject. It was probably inevitable that when his army career began in 1942 he would be put into an intelligence role, and then come to Britain with Bill Bundy's team.

---

14 Paul K. Whitaker quoted by Thomas Parrish in *The Ultra Americans*, p. 101.

As the war came to a close, Norland found himself among a team of cryptanalysts sent to Germany to find out what codebreaking expertise the Germans had amassed, and to interrogate Germany's own codebreakers. On 23 May 1945, his group stumbled upon a find of immense size and even greater significance: 12 chests of equipment which the Germans had been using to intercept and decrypt Russian teleprinter signals, weighing about 7,500 kg (seven and a half tons). Norland had to accompany this precious, and highly secret, cargo back to Britain. It was an early strike in the Cold War, which was beginning even while the USSR was still allied to America.

Norland received the MBE and joined the NSA after the war, where he worked even after he 'retired' in 1974.

The culture shock for Americans arriving at Bletchley could be extreme. There was the experience of British catering to cope with, as observed by Landis Gores, who arrived in 1944:

> *Officially the Dining Hall but almost universally termed the Cafeteria, it offered a characteristic self-service line in the centre with long tables and stubby light chairs branching into both wings and only lightly screened kitchen behind; its bill of fare was equally rudimentary with boiled beef, boiled potato, boiled cabbage, and steamed pudding for dessert topped by a yellow quasi-lemon sauce with coffee and milk for same available at the urns, the latter powdered of course, and bring your own saccharin.*

Even the mansion building itself could be rather hard to swallow:

> *Built about 1960 in an undiscriminatingly imitative Tudor vocabulary out of an endemic dark red brick with beige coadestone*

> *trim, quoins, voussoirs and keystones ... alongside oriels, turrets, bay windows and embrasures, all capped by myriad multi-potted chimneys in totally wanton location and configuration could only hulk into view as altogether inchoate, unfocused and incomprehensible, not to say indigestible.*

Over the coming weeks the American arrivals were immersed, if not drowned, in the lore of Enigma. They were part of Hut 3 – now located in its spanking new, though unprepossessing, brick and concrete block. Hut 3 thus had a new division, Hut 3-US, whose job was to liaise between Bletchley and Washington. Routeing intelligence via Washington was an inefficient way to get the news to General Eisenhower, though, so their mission soon evolved into a distribution as well as intelligence function, supplying indoctrinated intelligence officers to the tactical commands. Intelligence officers were sent from Hut 3 to join Eisenhower's land and air forces, to act as a bridge between the production of Ultra intelligence and the users in the field.

Landis Gores (1919–91)

Landis Gores was an architect. His light, comfortable buildings avoid the aggression of postwar brutalism, being modern and simple, yet human. His reaction to the kaleidoscopic architectural confection that was the mansion building at Bletchley is hardly surprising, though Gores' characteristically gothic writing style makes it seem like a horror, a judgement with which a modern visitor would probably disagree.

Although only at Bletchley for just over a year, Gores wrote his own memoir about the place – 769 pages of exorbitant purple prose, giving the tiniest (and, in the final judgement, fascinating) details about his colleagues, his work and his surroundings. It is a wonder that his book is so different from his buildings.

Gores himself was educated at Princeton (coincidentally studying there at the same time as Alan Turing was working for his PhD degree) and Harvard. In 1942, Gores joined the US Army, found himself at Bletchley Park, and spent the war in Hut 3 (by then located in a new brick building called Block D). Despite the apparent disparity between his vocation and his war job, Gores made a good enough interpreter of decrypts to end the war with a Legion of Merit award and an OBE.

After the war his career as an architect began to take off – until in 1954 he was struck down with polio. Clients found it hard to imagine that their building could be designed by a man in a wheelchair, but his talent enabled him to overcome prejudice. His family house is now listed on the US National Register of Historic Places.

Not cricket

Still, the tensions relating to who could see what had not entirely gone away. The trouble was leaks. During 1942, it had become apparent to the British that American appreciations concerning the North African theatre, destined for Washington, had been intercepted and read by the Germans. Later, in August 1943, another decrypt at Bletchley suggested that an unnamed, highly-placed official in the US Naval Department had informed the Abwehr that U-boat signals were being read by the Allies. The same month, General George V. Strong, from the outset a supporter of Anglo-American signals intelligence cooperation, visited Bletchley Park. On his agenda was an interview with Commander Travis' cold-steel executive, Nigel de Grey (see pages 32–3, Chapter 1).

The Gores Pavilion, a building designed in the clean style characteristic of architect (and codebreaker) Landis Gores.

When he emerged from the meeting, General Strong had agreed that there was, in fact, no need to send the output of Hut 3 to Washington at all; sending the material straight to the front, insofar as the fighting generals needed to know, was quite sufficient. Of course, Washington would get a summary update every so often. Indeed, the good General had been ambushed.

Strong returned to Washington, where there was music to face. It did not take long to dismantle the Strong-de Grey accord; alongside the 6813th Bletchley Park now had the 6812th Signals Intelligence Detachment, which were to be in charge of a section of British bombes dedicated to American work. There began a flow of American service personnel, making the Americans less of a curiosity and more into colleagues. Welcome colleagues: fresh American coffee made for instant friendships, and transatlantic alliances blossomed into weddings in a few cases.

Cultural barriers could be overcome. Selmer Norland was a star baseball pitcher. Rounders had been played on the lawn at Bletchley during the first summer of 1940, so efforts to teach baseball to the British were not wholly unsuccessful. Norland's colleague Paul K. Whitaker thought that the British coped better with the round bat of baseball than the Americans adapted to the British counter-blast, which was to introduce them to cricket. Apparently, the rules of baseball included etiquette such as 'interfering with a fielder attempting to catch a ball by spiking, kicking, pinching or goosing him lays the interferer open to a slug on the kisser' and 'in eye-gouging, only one thumb per eye is allowed.' Even though the 'rules' were a joke, by comparison, cricket may have seemed somewhat prim. The enduring problem in cricket was to remember to carry the bat when running between the wickets.

Meanwhile, back in Washington, there was to-and-fro of a different kind. Some very large cash registers were unloaded on 12 September 1943 from a railroad car which had made an overnight journey from Dayton, Ohio. Just looking at the size of the packing cases was probably enough to suggest that they might not contain cash registers at all,

Codebreakers playing rounders in the grounds of Bletchley Park early in World War II.

despite the NCR branding. These were the first six Desch bombes. Every week, another train would arrive with another six bombes, until a full 120 of the semi-electronic machines had been installed. They were operated by WAVES – Women Accepted for Voluntary Emergency Service, America's equivalent to the Wrens. There were WAVES at Dayton as well as at Arlington Hall – and estimates suggest that over 10,000 WAVES worked in codebreaking roles. As in Britain, American women were going into battle against the four-rotor Enigma to beat the U-boats.

As it happened, the British had not been completely sidelined in the development of machinery to tackle the four-rotor Enigma. They had had a slow start, but four-rotor bombes were also in operation at the Bletchley Park outstations. These were the result, not just of inventiveness in Britain, but also of rivalry and dissent. Bletchley Park had gone through another civil war, but machinery was now the main force in the battle of the codes.

CHAPTER 8
Machine Minds

Eighteen months had passed from the point where the codebreakers of Bletchley Park knew they would need a four-rotor bombe to read U-boat Enigma, and yet there was still no sign of such a thing. It wasn't for want of trying: indeed, it might have been that everyone was trying too hard.

Initially, the decision was taken to allow the BTM factory in Letchworth, which was doing sterling work turning out three-rotor bombes, to focus on that, rather than get distracted with a new and complex engineering project. The four-rotor solution needed to be an addition to the standard three-rotor machine, and Commander Travis thought he had found just the man and the resources to create the supplementary device that was needed.

C.E. Wynn-Williams was a Welsh-speaking engineer who was working on radar at the Telecommunications Research Establishment. In 1931 he had published a seminal paper on the use of 'thyratrons' for automated high-speed counting. Thyratrons were a type of gas-filled tube, closely related to the valves or vacuum-tubes being used as switches in other electronics experiments, notably by Joe Desch in the United States. Inventiveness was converging around electronics.

Curiously, the fourth-rotor solution being considered by Wynn-Williams was a mechanical device. It would have a shaft spinning at 2,000 rpm to create and break the extra 26 electrical connections implied by the fourth rotor. Unless the bombe was going to be slowed down to an unacceptable plod, these connections would have to be made and broken at least 400 times a second. It was going to be very delicate indeed, since dust or vibration could break a connection or cause a short-circuit. Driving electromechanical technology at these speeds was pushing machinery to its very limits. The new device would have to be shielded from the bombe itself; through a hole in the wall a fat snaking black cable would connect the two devices together. Because of this, the machine was called the cobra.

Wynn-Williams' brilliance showed less in the design of the cobra, which was not much of a success at first – the connections would 'bounce' at the high speed demanded – but in the 'sensing' mechanism to see if a correct or plausible solution to the Enigma settings had been found. The whole point of a bombe is to stop at a combination of rotor-positions which could have been used by the operator to send his encrypted message, so the 'sensing' mechanism needed to be super-fast as well, with 400 or more positions whizzing past every second. The Wynn-Williams solution was to use electronic valves to make a sensing unit which could switch upon detection of a stop far faster than any mechanical component – in fact, the solution which Joe Desch was working on in Dayton, Ohio. His unit was ready in the autumn of 1942, but the delays and problems with the cobra meant that it could not be put to the test.

The plan was for the special Wynn-Williams electronic sensing unit to be built by the Post Office. The Post Office had been experimenting with making switching at telephone exchanges electronic: they had the capability, and what's more they had access to electronic valves in sufficient numbers. And that's when things started to go wrong.

A high-speed spin

The electronics team at the Post Office Research Station, located at Dollis Hill in North London, was headed by Tommy Flowers. Flowers was a master of electronic engineering, and once the problem had been explained to him, he could immediately see what was needed. In other words, he decided to design a sensing-unit of his own. Now there were two competing models for the device, even though there was not yet a four-rotor bombe on which to test them.

Tommy Flowers (1905–98)

Without Tommy Flowers' ambition and self-confidence the story of Bletchley Park, and the story of computing in Britain, could have been very different. It's said that, aged five, on learning of the birth of his sister, Flowers remarked that he would have preferred a Meccano set. On leaving school, Flowers was apprenticed to learn the craft of mechanical engineering at the Royal Arsenal in Woolwich. But this was not enough: in 1922 he enrolled in a course of evening study to get a degree in electrical engineering. On graduation in 1926, he joined the General Post Office, and transferred to their research arm at Dollis Hill in 1930.

His doggedness in building the valve-based Colossus machine came at personal cost. After the war, the government made him an *ex-gratia* award of £1,000, but this did not even cover Flowers' personal investment in purchasing the equipment he had used to build Colossus. It is also said that Flowers applied for a bank loan to build an electronic computing machine, but was turned down as the bank refused to believe such a machine could be constructed. The tyranny of the Official Secrets Act meant that Flowers could not tell the bank that several already existed.

Flowers was a survivor. When, eventually, the veil began to lift on the Colossus project in the 1990s, Flowers was its principal advocate, explaining to the public what had happened and its relevance to computer development. Yet, whenever a newspaper story is run about Colossus and computers at Bletchley, there is still a muddle: there is usually an irrelevant picture of an Enigma machine, and the story of Lorenz and its much vaster complexity, and Flowers' achievement, is pushed onto the sidelines.

In fact, it was even more complicated. Harold (Doc) Keen, the loyal chief engineer of BTM, had been working on a sensing unit of his own, entirely with the knowledge and blessing of Bletchley Park. His unit was called the Mammoth, and its job was to test multiple cross-pluggings. (The basic bombe as designed by Turing and Welchman found possible settings for the three rotors, and one out of the ten possible cross-pluggings; then a manual process was needed to weed out 'wrong stops' which threw out inconsistencies in the other cross-pluggings. It was impossible for 'C' to be plugged to 'X' if it was supposed to be plugged to 'R' – and the Mammoth was designed to do this sort of weeding automatically.) So, there were now three sensing unit solutions being worked on. And if that wasn't complicated enough, Doc Keen had also been aware of the four-rotor question from the beginning, and he reckoned he could create a fast four-rotor bombe which didn't need a cobra. Keen had an idea for a fast electromechanical relay which could work at the speeds required, with good reliability – all he needed to do was to slow down the fast rotors on the three-rotor bombe, just a little, to get his system to work.

Harold (Doc) Keen (1894–1973)

Doc Keen was a pianist, and towards the end of his teenage years he was appointed as organist at St John's Church,

Tommy Flowers, whose vision for an electronic memory for Colossus anticipated computing technology of the post-war era.

Hoxton, which is close to the modern 'silicon roundabout' at Old Street in London. But his career lay in engineering, and in particular the crossover between mechanical engineering and electricity. His entire career was spent at BTM, its predecessor and successor companies.

In World War I there was an interlude while Keen served with the Royal Flying Corps, where he gained yet more experience, this time with engines. His imagination and ability to create new designs – over 60 patents in the interwar years – led to him becoming BTM's Chief Engineer and Head of Design and Development. At the end of World War II, he was awarded the OBE (the chairman of BTM received a knighthood, as is the way of things). In 1973, as the Enigma story was beginning to break into public knowledge, he was approached to write his own account of the bombe project. The answer was no, since even Keen was embargoed by the Official Secrets Act.

Why 'Doc' Keen? He carried his tools and papers and other bits and pieces around in a doctor's bag – a neat compromise between a workman's tool-box and a professional's briefcase. So, his fellow engineers called him 'Doctor' Keen, and it stuck.

In the winter of 1942–3, the Dollis Hill sensing unit became ready for testing. A bombe machine named *Freemantle* was taken off codebreaking duty and released to Flowers and his colleagues for that purpose. In carrying out their tests, they changed the drive mechanism of *Freemantle's* fast rotors, and failed to lubricate one of the crucial gear-wheels in the machine. The result was that *Freemantle* seized up and was put out of action for six weeks. The codebreakers were furious.

If all that was not bad enough, the inauspicious start of the relationship between Bletchley Park and the Post Office was just about to get

Harold 'Doc' Keen was the engineer who brought the Turing-Welchman bombe concept into reality and was the loyal supporter of GC&CS throughout the war.

worse. Flowers, and his boss Dr W.G. Radley, were pushing hard for their electronic sensing solution. It wasn't just a question of their sensing-unit being preferred over Wynn-Williams' design: now the threat to their project was coming from Keen and his high-speed relays. Bizarrely, in view of their ham-fistedness with *Freemantle*, Flowers and Radley asserted that they knew more about relays and mechanical engineering than the highly-experienced Keen, they said that the high-speed four-rotor Keen bombe was bound to fail, and urged Bletchley to ditch Keen.

This was a bit much for Gordon Welchman, who had had to take time out from his principal duties as head of Hut 6 to sort out the wars between the engineers. He had worked with Keen on many problems for over three years and respected his judgement and versatility. Keen's four-rotor prototype had been tested and was known to work: Dr Radley's rant was out of place. Something would have to be done, and if Welchman were in charge, Bletchley Park would never have anything to do with the Post Office again.

As with many difficult diplomatic problems at Bletchley Park, this tricky situation found its way to the office of Nigel de Grey, the ice-cold fixer at Travis' right hand. Radley was confronted by the nonsense he had uttered. The risk of not doing any work for Bletchley, with its high demand for cutting-edge technology, was real. Radley backed down quickly. Fortunately for Radley and Flowers, Travis himself was keen to keep the Post Office engineers on board, and eventually the problems resolved themselves.

Bletchley Park's outstations began to receive high-speed four-rotor bombes built to Keen's specification in the spring of 1943. Eventually 56 of these machines would be brought into service, and their reliability was never in doubt. But the cobra was not dropped. The 'bouncing' problem of electrical contacts at high speed was eventually solved and 13 of these huge machines were brought into service too. Electronic sensing was proven, not just in Britain but also in America, and the day of the valve was about to dawn. But first, there was another problem, and it also involved machines.

Hollerith's legacy

As the 'wicked uncles' letter episode demonstrated, Gordon Welchman could disregard the chain of command when it was necessary, and point out unpleasant truths to those in power. Fortunately, he had a strong enough relationship with his ultimate boss, Commander Travis, for it to be reasonably safe for him to send a mildly critical note to Travis about the four-rotor bombe fiasco. Prudently, Welchman had been through it all (including writing a close-typed ten-page blow-by-blow account) with Nigel de Grey first. Travis might have been somewhat more surprised, a few weeks later, to receive another closely-typed memo in which the dismay and lost pride explodes from the very first paragraph.

This one was not written by Welchman, and it was all about the insensitivity of the very person Travis had come to rely on – none other than Nigel de Grey. It was from Frederic Freeborn, the head of the Bletchley Park Hollerith machine section, and the outrage was all because de Grey had asked whether Mr Freeborn (for that is what he was called, by everyone, without exception) 'had one or two particular girls that [Freeborn] could fully trust to handle such vital documents'.

Frederic Freeborn (1897–1977)

Always known as 'Mr Freeborn' (no first name, no nickname), Freeborn came across as a slightly remote, controlling, and possibly forbidding figure to the much younger staff who had to go to Block C and ask for a mechanized solution to one of the many routine codebreaking tasks demanding patience, repetition on a huge scale, and accuracy. 'He was a business man and always in a business suit. Every discussion I had about the work to be done for us was with Mr Freeborn himself and he was in total command of the detail. I always went to his office in Block C, never he to mine.'[15]

Nevertheless, Freeborn could put on a show when needed, notably when Churchill came to visit in 1941. The machines (then in Hut 7) were coordinated to start and stop simultaneously, for short bursts, while the PM was shown around. At the end of the display all machines broke out into a form of mechanical applause. One senses that the great man was impressed – as was Mr Freeborn's secretary, who snuck Churchill's cigar butt out of the ashtray to keep it as a treasured souvenir.

Freeborn was a graduate of the University of London, whose talents were not simply organizational. Organizing the Hollerith machine operation was, in fact, a form of computer programming, though the phrase had not been invented then. What is more, it required specialist engineering expertise, since the machines needed to be adapted to meet the peculiar demands of Bletchley Park. Behind the business suit lay a powerful intellect. Freeborn finished the war with an OBE and transferred from BTM to GCHQ on a permanent basis, continuing his efficient operation.

Herman Hollerith died in 1929 so cannot claim to be a Bletchley Park codebreaker. But he was the pioneer whose punched-card sorting and tabulating technology was at the heart of Bletchley Park's largest wartime on-site machine section. Since the earliest days of 1940 there

15 Edward Simpson in Ralph Erskine and Michael Smith (eds.), *The Bletchley Park Codebreakers* (2011), p. 139.

The Freebornery punch room at Bletchley Park.

had been a dedicated team of programming experts and engineers, led by Freeborn and two brothers, Ronald and Norman Whelan, from the BTM company, permanently on the site. First, they had been in Hut 7, which had grown since 'being a wooden structure it had been comparatively easy for workmen to tear down walls and partitions, and to tack on extensions, not once but several times', though by late 1942 this expedient had reached its limits and the machinists had moved into a new brick building, Block C.

By this stage everybody knew the drill. 'Some of the cryptanalytical departments had a tendency to tell Freeborn how to use his machines in support of each problem,' wrote Welchman many years later; 'of course not all the cryptanalytic sections made the mistake of dictating to Freeborn.' Edward Simpson observed that if you made that mistake, or if you just came to Freeborn under-prepared, your job would probably go to the back of the queue. This made for some tensions, but nobody would doubt the integrity of Freeborn or his staff, even if they were from BTM. De Grey had blundered.

Hollerith machinery was used in a huge variety of ways at Bletchley, which perhaps makes it surprising that it is rarely mentioned and even more rarely described in the literature about codebreaking. Initially, BTM (which had a franchise agreement with IBM in the United States to exploit Hollerith's patents and to make machines which, in essential features, replicated IBM's designs) had brought one of its own tabulators to Bletchley, but this could not print alphabetical characters, so they dug an IBM model 405 out of storage and found that this was much more versatile and suited to the range of jobs that Freeborn and his team were being asked to do. More 405s were ordered – with the pleasant surprise on arrival that the Americans had packed gifts of food among the kit, 'giving us among other items our first introduction to Spam.'

The machines assisted the attack on Naval Enigma. One challenge was to work out which rotors were in the right-hand and middle positions of the Enigma machine, since this cut down the number of runs required on the very limited number of bombes at the disposal of the naval codebreakers. A partial solution was to find 'depths' – the jargon-word meaning several messages sent using the same or related settings. Searching for repeated sequences of letters (such as 'tetras', runs of four letters which cropped up in more than one message) was just the sort of task suited to automation on punched-card machines. Another job, in breaking Japanese codes, was to print 'Indexes of Good Groups': the codebreakers painstakingly identified the code words, comprising groups of typically five numbers, but these needed to be sorted into usable printed indexes in numerical order to be of use for reading messages. Much codebreaking uses modular arithmetic (where you do not 'carry' tens, so that 7 + 9 = 6) and again punched cards could do this conveniently, accurately and fast. Breaking the Italian Hagelin cipher machine was perhaps the most demanding task for the Freebornery, as the Hollerith section became known: 'it was a very large job, and quite complicated, requiring a large number of operators. It was the only job where we found it necessary to lay down chalk lines on the machine room floor to ensure correct sequence movement of boxes of cards to the various machines involved.'[16] In addition, the Freebornery handled the Central Index – where the microscopic details of German officers, ships, locations, units, technical data and more were collected – and it had responsibility for producing Britain's own top security one-time-pad cipher sheets.

The scale of the operation was huge. Daily, the Enigma messages being processed involved around 80,000 characters, which had to be punched onto cards. Collating 'tetras' used around 84,000 cards, with some cards passing through the machines several times. The sorting machines could process 400 cards a minute, yet a 'tetras' job could consume as much as 100 machine-hours. The machine-room had 300 staff, including 200 Wrens, working five shifts, and the working

16 Marjorie Halcrow, quoted by Michael Smith in *The Secrets of Station X* (2011), p. 110.

conditions were challenging: 'The main room contained [large] machines, about the size of a small piano, called the sorting machines which could read the cards and sort the hundreds of thousands of messages into different categories. There were loads of sorters and there were collating machines that were even larger. The whole department was filled with machinery. It was a very noisy place, all banging on all night and day long.' It is estimated that the number of cards used was two million, representing a six-ton lorryload of card stock, every week.

Mr Welchman's Section

Machines were click-clacking and throbbing their way into everything going on at Bletchley Park. The age of squared-paper seemed to be over. Travis must have realized, with all the goings-on about the bombe, and now with Freeborn taking umbrage at the apparent slight unintentionally perpetrated by Nigel de Grey, that something needed to be done about the organization of machine usage and development at Bletchley Park.

> *I am setting up a new Section under Mr Welchman to deal with all matters arising from the development of new machinery as an aid to Cryptography. It will be known as the Machine Co-ordination and Development Section. Mr Welchman should be consulted on all questions of machine aids (other than the BTM machines in Mr Freeborn's Section). … He should not in any way interfere with the very close liaison which exists between Mr Freeborn and the various Sections.*
>
> *He will call together a Committee, which should meet at least once a month, and of which I wish the following to be members:-*
>
> *Mr Welchman (Chairman)*
> *Professor Vincent*
> *Messrs Newman, Turing, Freeborn, Wynn-Williams and Major Morgan…*

Mr Milner-Barry will become head of Hut 6 and I hope Mr Welchman will be able to keep a fatherly eye on the progress of his old section and be called in for consultation if and when advisable.

E.W. Travis *10th September, 1943*

Although Travis was reacting to a trend as well as a tendency to grumble among his machine-dependent sections, there was a new project which was going to consume a vast amount of machinery, and Travis had recently given it the go-ahead. This was the brainchild of Alan Turing's mentor and former lecturer at Cambridge, whose name appears in Travis' list of committee members – M.H.A. Newman. Newman was going to rehabilitate the reputation of the Post Office at Bletchley Park, but more significantly, he was going to bring Bletchley, and the world at large, into the computer age, and in so doing he would uncover the contents of Adolf Hitler's most personal, most strategic and most secret communications. M.H.A. Newman was a professor of the extraordinary type, who had been put onto the problem of Fish.

M.H.A. (Max) Newman (1897–1984

Max (to his friends) Newman was born in London; his father had emigrated from Bromberg, then part of Germany (now Bydgoszcz, in Poland), and his surname was Neumann when Max was born. On the outbreak of World War I, his father was interned and returned to Germany; Max and his mother changed their name, and Max did war duty in various forms. At Cambridge he excelled in mathematics and was elected fellow of St John's College in 1923.

Newman's career from Cambridge onwards is an anticipation, or a mirror, of that of Alan Turing. His most famous pupil was indebted to Newman for the mentoring and guidance which he provided for all of Turing's adult life. Newman taught Turing at Cambridge, leading Turing to the most important mathematical discovery of Turing's career, embodied in the seminal paper *On Computable Numbers*. Turing went on to teach Newman's own course on the foundations of mathematics at Cambridge; both spent substantial time at Princeton in the US; both wound up at Bletchley; both spent the final active years of their careers at the University of Manchester. In all these things they collaborated, and in all of them except the move to Bletchley Park Max Newman led the way. It is clear that Alan Turing's breakthrough ideas in mathematics, computing, developmental biology and more were all highly influenced by Newman. Described as 'a man of deep culture and sensitivity', Newman was musical and shared a dry sense of humour with his pupil. His ability to see beyond the peculiarities of Alan Turing enabled them to have a close personal relationship, and for Newman (and his wife, the writer Lyn Irvine) to provide support and, by proxy, some sort of family for Turing.

Newman himself accumulated a far more impressive array of awards than Turing: Fellow of the Royal Society, president of the London Mathematical Society and of the Mathematical Association, recipient of the De Morgan Medal, an honorary fellowship of St John's and an honorary doctorate. He turned down the OBE he was offered on leaving Bletchley.

The filleting of Fish

In 1940, the 'Y Service' – the radio-monitoring service whose job was to scan the airwaves and capture the secret wireless signals – had detected

M.H.A. (Max) Newman, mentor of Alan Turing, and leader of the machine attack on Lorenz ciphers.

a new kind of traffic. Unlike Morse Code, with its staccato dots and dashes, this was more of a continuous chirrup. It was soon realized that the signals were in the Baudot-Murray Code used for teleprinters, which allocates five binary digits to each letter, so A becomes 11000, B 10011, C 01110 and so on. A '1' would be transmitted as an impulse and a 0 would be silent. Teleprinter transmissions were fast and automated, and they were very much longer than Enigma messages. At Bletchley Park, this kind of traffic was code-named 'Fish'. Different networks, using different distinguishing characteristics, were named after different fish: bream, codfish, turbot, jellyfish and so on.

The only problem was that the teleprinter messages which had been intercepted were enciphered, and nobody knew what the device for encipherment was. What was evident was that some kind of arithmetical cipher – an overlay of some apparently random string of 1s and 0s – had been added to the original message to disguise it. As with all cipher-breaking, the question was what this string, this key, actually was, and how it was generated. This kind of problem was never one to daunt John Tiltman, who was presented on 30 August 1941 with a priceless gift: a duplicated message, where the sender had re-transmitted the same signal but, on the second attempt, had got bored and introduced abbreviations and shortcuts which were not in the original. This not-quite copying gave Tiltman his way in, exploiting the peculiarities of binary arithmetic.

If you add 1 and 1 in binary, with non-carrying addition, you get 0. If you add 0 and 0, you also get 0. So, if the two messages presented to Tiltman were added together, all that would result is a long string of 0s – except where the operator had varied the text. Each point of variance, signalled by a 1 in the added-messages string, gave Tiltman a weak point: here he could guess at the original and abbreviated forms, and try them out against the two texts. As the same key had been used for both messages, soon the original text could be unzipped from the two intercepts, and the key would incidentally be revealed.

Tiltman's achievement at unravelling the duplicated message did not tell the Allies anything of tactical value, but what it had done is provide a long string of key which the codebreakers could work on. In October 1941, a Cambridge science and mathematics student called Bill Tutte was sent off to do what he could. 'For all that time, I saw him staring into the middle distance for extended periods, twiddling his pencil and making endless counts on reams of paper for nearly three months, and I used to wonder whether he was getting anything done,' said Jerry Roberts, who joined Bletchley Park in 1941 to work on teleprinter traffic. It turned out that Bill Tutte certainly was getting something done.

Tutte saw that the 'indicator' – the information sent by the message sender to tell the recipient how to set up his equipment for automatic decipherment – had some peculiarities. One was that part of it seemed only to use 23 of the possible 25 letters of the alphabet (the Germans used the same character for I and J in indicators). Maybe part of the machine had only 23 possible settings? 'In the cryptographical school in London we often attacked our simulated cipher messages by writing them out on some period that seemed appropriate. ... But what period should I use? That information about the indicators suggested that 23 might be worth trying.'[17] It worked. With more analysis of this kind, Tutte managed to tease out the fundamentals of the unknown machine.

Bill Tutte (1917–2002)

Unlike the typical codebreakers of World War I school, Tutte came from a relatively obscure background: his father

17 Bill Tutte in Jack Copeland, *Colossus: The Secrets of Bletchley Park's Codebreaking Computer* (2006), appendix 4.

was an estate gardener and his mother a cook, working in Newmarket in racing stables. At school he developed a passion for chemistry, and though he read mathematical texts and got himself interested in graph theory it was to read Natural Sciences – with a focus on chemistry – that Tutte went to Cambridge. Nonetheless he became close friends with the mathematicians he met there, and soon after graduating he was publishing papers on mathematical topics as well as chemistry.

It was the mathematics which brought him to Bletchley as the Oxbridge recruiting machine continued to spy out suitable candidates for a codebreaking role during the war. Within a few weeks of arriving he had unpeeled the Lorenz problem – an achievement of reverse engineering rightly described as one of the greatest intellectual feats of World War II.

When the war ended, he returned to Cambridge to complete his doctorate in mathematics, and in 1948 he was appointed to a post in Canada, where he spent the rest of his career. Only late in his life did his superlative work at Bletchley become known. In 2004, a memorial was erected in Newmarket to honour him and his achievement: a series of two-metre-high (six-and-a-half feet) stainless steel panels are punched with holes – but if you stand in the right place, the code comes together to create an image of Bill Tutte.

A fish called Tunny

In fact the unknown machine was called the Lorenz *Schlüsselzusatz* SZ40 (later models, SZ42). It was an attachment to a teleprinter which would automatically encrypt a message pre-typed by the operator – faster and slicker than Enigma, but a big heavy piece of equipment and not readily portable. It had 12 coding wheels, each of which had several pins around its circumference which could be set to 'on' or 'off'. Five coding wheels were needed to transform the five binary digits making up each character of the teleprinter alphabet; in fact, the Lorenz machine had two banks of five wheels, allowing for two transformations to disguise the plain text. As the wheels rotated, if a pin in the 'on' position made an electrical contact the binary digit 1 would be added to the signal: the letter A, ordinarily 11000, encountering a pin in the on-position in the fourth place, becomes 11010, or J. Tutte figured out this arrangement, and recognized that the two remaining wheels of the 12 were controlling the stepping motion of the second bank of five wheels. In summary, what he gleaned was:

- The machine had two banks of five coding wheels.
- One set of wheels, which were named 'chi' wheels by the codebreakers, moved on one step all together every time a new character was keyed into the teleprinter.
- The other set of wheels, called the 'psi' wheels, moved on only when told to by the two movement-controlling wheels. This characteristic was hugely helpful to the codebreakers, because the effect of the 'psi' wheels on two or more successive letters of the message was often identical – and using binary addition, the psi wheels' influence could be zeroed out.
- The number of pin positions on the wheels was curious, but was a security feature introduced by the Germans to make the 'period' of the key very long: the chi wheels had 41, 31, 29, 26 and 23 pins, and the psi wheels had 43, 47, 51, 53 and 59 pins. The motor wheels had 37 and 61. Tutte's period analysis had squeezed these numbers out of the intercepted traffic.

Now the codebreakers had it: not exactly a machine – they never saw one until the end of the war – but the structure of it; and they could go and build one to do their own deciphering. The machine they built was

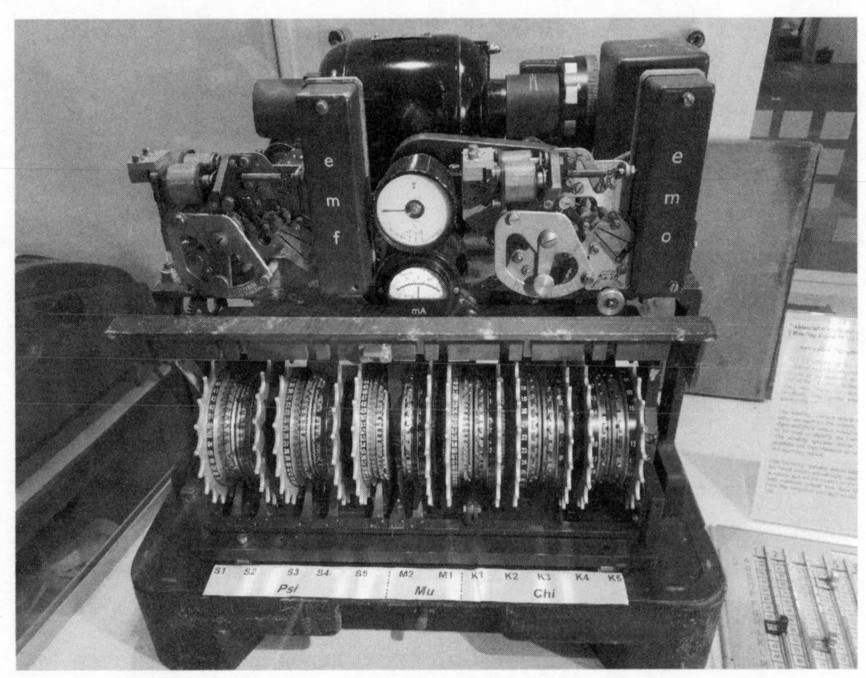

A Lorenz SZ42 machine, which enciphered teleprinter messages automatically.

called 'Tunny' – the British-English word in use in the 1940s for what the Americans called tuna.

Having a Tunny machine was all very well, but the problem of machine set-up – the same problem they had been wrestling with with Enigma since the beginning of the war – was still there. With the Lorenz machine, there were millions upon millions more ways of setting the pins on those code-wheels than there were set-ups of Enigma. But without knowing how the machine was set up, there was no simple way to decipher the teleprinter messages whirring through the air.

Once again Bill Tutte came up with an idea. Having discussed the Tunny problem with Alan Turing, he found a statistical method for finding the start positions of the coding wheels. If you added together adjacent letters of the intercepted message, that would (like as not) eliminate the effect of the psi wheels. Furthermore, it was possible to exploit the characteristics of German language to eliminate the plain-text (by binary addition) and thereby expose the effect of the chi wheels. German has a preponderance of digraphs like EI and CH and EN, and – once again – if you added together adjacent letters of plain German, in teleprinter code, the first two binary digits had a preponderance of 0s. Almost 60 per cent 0s. What the codebreakers had to do was match up the stream of 1s and 0s generated by the first two chi-wheels and test it against the first two binary digits of the adjacent-letters-added intercept, and look for a match giving 60 per cent 0s rather than completely random 1s and 0s. To carry out these numerous and repetitious calculations would require something more than manpower, even with the brains of someone like Bill Tutte.

Major Tester's team

While Tutte's statistical method was still nothing more than a theory, the challenge of the Tunny messages was not being disregarded. A new section was set up at Bletchley Park, headed by Major Ralph Tester, and as was the way of things at Bletchley, the unit was soon called the 'Testery'.

Ralph Tester (1902–98)

Ralph Tester was an accountant who worked in Germany before the war for Unilever. At Bletchley Park, he was an administrator: 'an urbane pipe smoker, about 40 years old, no cryptographer, nor did he pretend to be.'[18] So, it is not surprising to see him described as 'a shadowy figure, neither much encouraging nor admonishing'.[19] Glory is not often awarded for steering a steady course. After the end of World War II, Tester went back to Unilever, where he stayed for the rest of his working life.

Yet Tester had his moment of danger. On the way out of Germany in 1938 he was sharing a train with a group of refugees escaping from Czechoslovakia, shepherded by a lady Quaker. She persuaded Tester to conceal a small black notebook. The German police searched the train but Tester had hidden the book successfully, so that he could hand it to the Czech Refugee Organization in London on his arrival, even though the refugees had been thrown out of the train on the Dutch border and their fate was unknown. It turned out that the book contained the details of the Czechoslovak Communist Party; if Tester had been found with this on him, the consequences were unthinkable.

At the close of the war, as a German speaker with an understanding of complex machine encryption systems, Tester was included in the 'TICOM' teams sent to Germany to investigate what success the Germans had had in

18 Jerry Roberts, *Lorenz*, p. 48.
19 Roy Jenkins in Copeland, *Colossus*, p. 260.

breaking Allied codes. In the second week of May 1945 his team took possession of a captured convoy of four German signal trucks. These comprised Field Marshal Kesselring's communications unit, and included a Lorenz SZ42 machine – the very thing Tester's team had worked on, unseen, for four years.

Recruitment of codebreakers for the Testery was the usual Bletchley mix of university students and Wrens; Jerry Roberts described the somewhat haphazard process.

> *In trying to foresee how useful a person might be at breaking ciphers, the recruiters saw as promising an affection for chess or crosswords. Both Peter Ericsson and myself were put through this hoop when interviewed at the War Office by a Major Masters. It went:*
>
> *Masters: Do you play chess at all?*
>
> *Roberts: Oh yes, I enjoy chess.*
>
> *Masters: Do you tackle crosswords, such as the ones in* The Times *or the* Observer?
>
> *Roberts: Oh yes, I have a go at them often.*
>
> *Ericsson's responses were:*
>
> *(Chess) Oh, no, I've never bothered with it.*
>
> *(Crosswords) Oh no, no, no, waste of time.*

Both Roberts and Ericsson were hired, and both became shift leaders in the Testery.

The principal tasks of the codebreakers in the Testery were to strip off the stream of 1s and 0s which had been put on by the chi and psi wheels of the Lorenz machine. To begin with, the indicator system being used by the Germans was insecure and 'the Testery read nearly every message from July to October 1942'.[20] Then the procedure was changed, making the job much tougher, but using 'depths' – two or more messages sent using the same settings – an unzipping technique, similar to that originally used by John Tiltman, could be used. Depths were quite common, for example when a transmission problem led the receiver to ask for a re-send. Peter Hilton joined the Testery in 1942 after training in the Royal Artillery (the Testery was a better place); he described the unzipping process, where the messages did not quite line up, as follows:

> *You would guess some word, I remember once I guessed the word* 'Abwehr'*, eight symbols [including the spaces either side] of one of the two messages. But the eight letters in the other message would have a space in the middle followed by* 'Flug'*. So then you would guess, well, that's going to be* 'Flugzeug' *– aircraft. So you get* 'zeug' *followed by a space and that gives you five more letters of the other message. So you keep extending and going backwards as well.*

Even after the introduction of machinery the Testery was kept in business. The machines could, most of the time, produce only partial solutions to the set-up of the Lorenz machine, and the codebreakers in the Testery were in demand to find the settings of the psi-wheels or the pin-settings on the chi-wheels.

Not everyone was brilliant at the codebreaking tasks. One recruit to the Testery was Roy Jenkins (see pages 228–9, Chapter 9), who explained that there were 'breakers', the elite, and 'setters', whose work demanded logic and precision, while the breakers did the kind of thing described by Hilton. 'The night shift for some strange reason was the longest – nine hours – and it was certainly the bleakest. I remember quite a few absolutely blank nights, when nothing gave and I went to a dismal breakfast having played with a dozen or more messages and completely failed with all of them. It was the most frustrating mental experience

20 Jack Copeland et al, op. cit., p. 157.

I have ever had, particularly as the act of trying almost physically hurt one's brain.'

The Newmanry

Another arrival on the Bletchley Park scene was Alan Turing's lecturer from Cambridge, M.H.A. Newman. Newman's name appears on Denniston's list of professors, but there is something of a mystery there: next to his name someone has written 'No' in red crayon (Who said No? Why?). Newman was not, therefore, among the early arrivals at Bletchley. Nevertheless, in 1942, the recruitment machinery at Cambridge was still in action, and Frank Adcock (see pages 28–9, Chapter 1) got in touch to tempt Newman to come to Bletchley. Temptation took two forms, 'work which would I think interest you and which is certainly important for the War' and 'a very nice billet in a modern house with constant hot water.' Newman arrived in the autumn of 1942, joining the Tunny team laboriously trying to unpeel text from teleprinter messages sent in depth. Newman did not find that the work interested him at all. But he did think that Tutte's statistical method had some potential, if the drudgery involved could be mechanized. Newman went to see Travis, with the idea of building a machine to sort out the Fish.

Travis was receptive, and the Telecommunications Research Establishment under Wynn-Williams was engaged to construct the new machine. The essence of it was counting the 1s and 0s in the messages and looking for that 60 per cent coincidence rate against the 1s and 0s in the 'chi-stream'. 1s and 0s were most easily represented by holes (and no-holes) in punched paper tape, long skeins of which needed to be spun past a photoelectric optical reader. Wynn-Williams's fast electronic counter could certainly do the job, but finding a way to get the tapes to move synchronously and at speed was challenging. The tiny spikes on the sprocket-wheel to keep the tapes in line tended to shred the paper and if the holes were not perfectly in line with the reader it might take the light from the wrong hole. The five-metre (16 ft) ribbons of tape were threaded across pulley wheels in a contraption (called a bedstead) which looked like an iron bed frame on its end, and the whole thing looked like a joke from a Heath Robinson drawing. So that's what the machine was named: Heath Robinson.

In the spring of 1943 the new machine was ready for a ceremonial switch-on in front of the Bletchley Park VIPs. A large resistor overloaded and smoke rose ominously from the machine. Despite the inauspicious start, it was able to read 2,000 characters a second as the tapes flew past the readers. Comparing the added-adjacent first two binary digits of a 2,000-character intercept against the first two binary digits of the expected chi-stream in every possible starting-position of the chi wheels took half an hour – something unimaginable if it had had to be done by hand.

Heath Robinson's centrepiece was the counting mechanism using Wynn-Williams' electronics. For that reason the counters and circuitry came from the Telecommunications Research Establishment, but they had concluded that the tape-driving mechanism and tape-reading components should be made by the Post Office. So, Dollis Hill was back in the game of providing equipment for Bletchley.

Tommy Flowers soon became aware of the project, and in characteristic fashion he could immediately see the potential for improvement. He reckoned it would be possible to do away with one of the tape-readers altogether, by putting the data on the second tape into the machine itself: by storing it electronically. This would, at a stroke, do away with the mechanical-engineering problem of tape synchronicity, and it would allow for a much faster rate of character-reading on the one remaining tape – but it would instead create an entirely new one, which was to do with the stability of electronic valves.

Wynn-Williams' approach had been to minimize the number of valves, because in his experience valves tended to fail. But Flowers had been using valves for years as well, in his large-scale automated telephone exchange systems, and knew the secret. You didn't move the machine using valves, and you didn't switch them off. For portable machinery such as Wynn-Williams had been designing, a small number of valves

The Colossus machine in action, tended by two women from the WRNS.

made sense, since reliability was bound to be lower. But Flowers knew that a big machine could be made reliable. He started work on a new design. It was huge – it had 1,600 valves – an immense number given the perception of unreliability of these crucial components. Working day and night, Flowers got his prototype working by December 1943; that was at Dollis Hill, but it was a success, and after re-assembly in Newman's section at Bletchley the new machine was in action the following month. It was named Colossus.

The intelligence derived from Lorenz decrypts, assisted by Colossus, made a crucial difference to the last stages of the war. Extra Colossi were ordered to help prepare for the intelligence deluge expected around the invasion of Europe scheduled for the late spring of 1944. New, more ambitious designs were created: the Mark 2 Colossus had 2,400 valves. By VE-day, in May 1945, ten Colossi were working at Bletchley Park.

All this machinery, on such a scale, needed a home. Given that M.H.A. Newman was in charge, the home was called the 'Newmanry', and it was located in one of the new buildings approximately on the site of the old mansion's maze. Like many sections at Bletchley, the Newmanry relied on Wrens to operate the machines. New recruits could be bewildered at their induction, as the following two accounts illustrate:

> *We were deposited in front of a hideous Victorian Manor. There was no one to meet us. The place was* weird. *There were weedy looking boffin types walking in pairs or on their own.... After an hour of waiting ... a bald-headed man wearing round, metal-framed utility spectacles approached us and introduced himself as Mr Newman. We followed him into Block F – the Newmanry. He sat us down at a long trestle table and began teaching us a new kind of mathematics and logic.*[21]

21 Caroline Caughey, quoted by Copeland op. cit., p. 160.

> *Mr Newman was a very quiet man, reserved and not at ease with girls. He walked up and down in front of us with his eyes on the ground, talking about a machine with twelve wheels. When he had gone we were none the wiser. Later we discovered that he thought we had been told what the section did.*[22]

Nonetheless, Newman won the affection of his staff. His approach was informal: use of first names among the team was encouraged, and ideas were welcomed from all, with a weekly open-house to hear them. A commemorative silver tankard was presented to him at the end of the war, inscribed 'To MHAN from the Newmanry, 1943–45'. It was an avuncular, if not paternalistic, set-up; it seems that the first-names informality might not have extended as far as Mr Newman himself.

Colossus and the Newmanry had made significant contributions to the intelligence picture in the final months of the war. Lorenz messages, sent at the highest echelons of Hitler's war machine, contained priceless appreciations of strategy and plans which could not be gleaned so easily from the day-to-day mundane traffic being sent in Enigma. Furthermore, the Enigma operation was under threat, as the Germans proposed to introduce radical new design features to the Enigma machine which could wipe out the effectiveness of the bombe attack on the cipher. The Newmanry, and its sophisticated high-speed machinery, was a sign of the future.

The future was clearly electronic, but more importantly, the future was programmable. The mathematicians in the Newmanry, and some non-mathematicians too, were fascinated by the machine which could change its task when the switch-panel was reconfigured. According to Flowers:

> *They wanted programmable logic – and we provided them with a big panel with a lot of keys on it and by throwing the keys they could – the mathematicians – could program the machine. The keys did the 'and' and 'or' functions ... they were like a lot of schoolboys with a new toy when we first gave it to them; they thought it so*

22 Dorothy Du Boisson, quoted by Copeland op. cit, p. 160.

wonderful they were playing with it for ages just to see what you could do with it.

What they were doing with it was to test its capabilities as a stored-program universal electronic computer, the first such device anywhere in the world. It is no surprise that after World War II ended, Alan Turing went to work at the National Physical Laboratory to design Britain's 'Automatic Computing Engine' (he wanted Flowers as well, but the Post Office would not let him go), and M.H.A. Newman used his new appointment as Fielden Professor of Mathematics at Manchester University to set up a computer laboratory, which Turing later joined. Newman's lab built its own prototype electronic stored-program computer which ran the first program ever (a simple factorization routine) in late 1948. In later years, one of Newman's assistants, a young classicist called Donald Michie, set up an Artificial Intelligence school at Edinburgh University. These achievements were the offspring of Bletchley Park, the birthplace of modern computing.

In 1983, Tommy Flowers looked back at his triumphal achievement with the Colossus. 'Cryptanalysts at Bletchley Park had been reading German messages that had been encoded on a machine called Enigma. Alan M. Turing was a leading figure in this activity, and he explained it to me and told me what the Post Office was required to do – something that presented no difficulties to a telephone engineer. The work was soon found not to be needed; had that been realized earlier (and there was some suspicion that it could have been), Dollis Hill might never have been involved with Bletchley Park.' Perhaps that was a slightly rosy way of remembering the events of 40 years before. It was remarkable that the Post Office's relationship with Bletchley had survived the trauma of the four-rotor bombe, but a gift to modern computer science that it did.

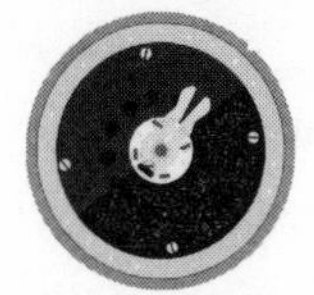 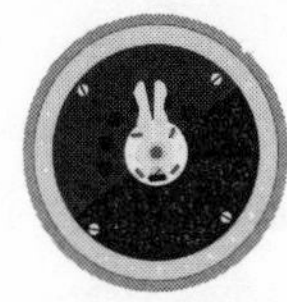 

CHAPTER 9
Breaking Up

It is tempting to think of D-Day as marking the end of the war: from here on, there seems to be an element of inevitability. Surely Germany was beaten; the plot against Hitler himself, engineered from within the internal German resistance, suggested that the path must surely be downhill for the Allies. Achieving the landings in Normandy without being pushed back into the sea looks, with all the advantages of hindsight, to be the first decisive step towards victory.

Perhaps so, but there was still a long way to go, and for the codebreakers at Bletchley there was no let-up in the intensity or importance of their work. For one thing, the success of the deception plan codenamed 'Fortitude South' had in part been verified through codebreaking: the Abwehr traffic handled in Peter Twinn's ISK section, the Fish material coming out of the Testery and the Newmanry, and the Japanese messages sent back from Baron Oshima to his superiors in Tokyo had all led to the same conclusion: that the German high command expected the invasion to take place across the Dover straits and not where it actually occurred. But even after the invasion, there was much to do. The Americans were now fighting on two fronts, in Italy as well as Normandy, to which a third would be added when the south of France was invaded. Enigma traffic was produced in large quantities, and needed to be sifted and processed for the commanders at these fronts. There was also the war against Japan, which was by no means over and largely unaffected by any continental war in Europe.

Then there were the V-weapons. Professor Norman (see pages 53–4, Chapter 2) was able to produce detailed evidence which added to the body of knowledge and understanding being disentangled in the highest quarters. It was slowly becoming clear that there would be a V-2 to follow the V-1, that the V-2 might be rocket-propelled, and that German technology had outreached the British ability to respond. There was no effective countermeasure – other than bombing the V-weapon launch sites... and codebreaking. By judicious use of the double-agents, working for the British but believed by the Germans to be loyal spies for the Fatherland, deception about the point-of-impact of the V-weapons could be fed back to the Germans, causing the flying bombs and rockets to under-shoot their targets. But ultimately it required the troops on the ground to overrun the launch sites before the menace could be quelled for good.

The theory of moving downhill, though, could have its unhappy moments. A tendency to overlook inconvenient signals intelligence had not been completely cured; one example was the indications of German tanks near the target zones to which the British paratroopers were headed in Operation MARKET GARDEN, Montgomery's attempt to steal a march and leapfrog across the Rhine – which notoriously ended in disaster. Then, at the end of 1944, the Germans achieved complete surprise in their own Operation WACHT AM RHEIN, a counter-offensive into Luxembourg and France across the Ardennes. The problem here was partly complacency (an American intelligence report began with the unfortunate comment 'The enemy has had it') but partly the very success of Ultra itself. While there was intelligence to suggest that the German army had one last push in mind, there was nothing to confirm that in the signals. The German army had imposed a new discipline on itself: complete silence. Without the validation of Ultra, the intelligence staff did not tell General Omar Bradley that anything unusual was afoot, and thus it was that the Americans were caught napping.

Nevertheless, the enemy *had* had it: the Ardennes offensive, now known as the Battle of the Bulge, was soon over, and the Allies marched on into Germany at the start of 1945, as the Red Army invaded from the east. By the spring it was all over, and the future of the codebreakers at Bletchley Park had to be decided.

Bombe disposal

Certainly there was still fighting in the Far East, and the Japanese sections at Bletchley had work to do. But the majority of staff had been working on European problems, and in particular there were hundreds of Wrens and others who had operated bombes in numbers which had no continuing purpose.

The parts were useful, possibly. Jenny Conduit joined the Wrens at the age of 17 in 1942 and was sent to work on the bombes at Stanmore, the huge outstation of Bletchley Park dedicated to finding the settings being used to encipher Enigma messages.

> *In 1945 the German war was over, and suddenly we were redundant. Watchkeeping ceased and we were set to work dismantling the bombes. I recall sitting at trestle tables unscrewing the drums. Gradually we were dispersed to other categories and I was drafted to Plymouth, a port at last! My job was helping to demobilize sailors … I had become very thin and tired after two and a half years watchkeeping, but after a few weeks in Plymouth with the sea air, much better food and regular hours I felt re-born and enjoyed my last year in the WRNS hugely and felt part of the Navy at last.*

The mixture of elation and deflation was common among the Wrens tasked with this new job. 'It had been a sin to drop a drum but now we were allowed to roll one down the floor of the hut!' And yet 'It was so strange. It was already nearly empty – a ghost town with just a few removal men shifting furniture. Thousands of people just walked out the gate never to return.'

M.H.A. Newman was equally interested to get his hands on redundant equipment. The Colossus machines were, on one view, as irrelevant as the bombes, and he put in a bid for the valves and other useful parts as a starter kit for his computing machine project at Manchester University, where he had just been appointed Fielden Professor of Mathematics. On 8 August 1945, Newman wrote to Nigel de Grey, saying 'After going round the equipment ... the proper request for us to make is for the material of two complete Colossi; and in addition a few thousand miscellaneous resistances and condensers off other machines.' Three months later, the shipment was on its way, a total of 7 tons of old kit. This provided the starter for Newman's computing project, which developed the 'Manchester Baby' computer, believed to be the first ever stored-program electronic computer to run a routine, in the autumn of 1948. That success tempted Alan Turing away from a different computing machine project, at the National Physical Laboratory, which was running into the sand. Turing was able to work on Manchester's Mark I computer, a much bigger machine not built out of Bletchley left-overs, and spent the final years of his life there using it for his groundbreaking work modelling the growth patterns of living things.

But not all the machinery was broken up. Enigma machines continued in use in East Germany until 1955, and American cryptanalytic efforts against the machine, using bombes, continued until then. Bombe decryption was finally terminated in the US during 1956. In 2018, GCHQ revealed that 50 bombes and 20 Enigma machines had been kept 'in deep storage', in case of future use of Enigma machines. The GCHQ stash of wartime machines was disposed of in 1959, bringing an end to the bombe story. Only one original bombe survived, which is a Joe Desch model four-rotor bombe, on display at the National Cryptologic Museum in Maryland.

TICOM

Preparation against the threat of new enemies took other forms beyond the retention of machinery and skills. Even before D-Day the British had begun thinking about German capabilities in various technical spheres, and codebreaking and signals intelligence was one area in which the Allies were particularly interested.

As preparations for the invasion began, the Americans got wind of the British idea of capturing Germans who had been working in signals intelligence. Soon they had recognized that 'special handling of German signal intelligence targets which may be overrun' would be 'particularly desirable'.[23] The project was covered by the acronym 'TICOM', which even written out in full was the equally obscure 'Target Intelligence Committee'. A list of 'subjects for inquiry' was drawn up, and GC&CS personnel, American as well as British, were selected to parachute into Germany with the 101st American Airborne Division, to grab their opposite numbers and their equipment. Although some of the Bletchley Park staff were in uniform, the prospect of leaping out of aircraft into enemy territory cannot have been very appealing to the codebreakers selected for the task. Fortunately, and no doubt partly because those who were cleared for Ultra intelligence were not supposed to be put into battle zones in case the captures were the reverse way round, the plan was changed. The first teams were sent in, behind the front line troops, in April 1945.

Art Levenson, one of the Americans at Bletchley, was sent in with one of the teams. 'When we left on the TICOM trip, this sergeant said, "Boy, the war must really be over if they're sending you guys."' His team was able to capture Field Marshal von Rundstedt's communications party, comprising six trucks full of radio receivers, encryption machinery, and the men who operated it.

TICOM Team 1 was led by Wing Commander Dr Oscar Oeser from Hut 3. One objective of the Team was an intact Lorenz machine – still of great interest despite, or possibly because of, the success against Fish traffic at Bletchley Park. By the second week of May 1945, they had caught the Fish: to be exact, the machine and all its associated ancillary units as used by Field Marshal Kesselring, in the link which Bletchley

23 SHAEF memo declassified by US Government.

had codenamed 'Jellyfish'. Jellyfish had been the vital Fish network during the period of the Normandy invasion, linking Paris and Berlin; Kesselring had taken over command in the west in March of 1945, long after France had been lost to the Germans, but the teleprinter equipment, and the characteristics of the link, had been retained as the German Army retreated.

Oscar Oeser (1904–83)

Oscar Oeser was born in Pretoria into a family of German Jewish immigrants. His academic career began with a degree in physics and mathematics; then he went to Marburg in Germany, getting a doctorate in psychology, then on to Trinity College, Cambridge, to pick up another doctorate in experimental psychology. With this forbidding array of degrees, Dr Dr Oeser went to teach at the most unorthodox boarding school in England, Dartington Hall (mixed-sex dormitories, no regular curriculum, free thought and behaviour, and no organized games) among whose pupils was the future Soviet spy Michael Straight. The unorthodox environment allowed Oeser to marry, divorce and remarry during the year or so that he was there.

Then he was off to St Andrews on what was to be a long and respected academic career in experimental psychology, a subject to which he attempted to impose mathematical discipline where empirical approaches could lead to wishy-washy thinking. After the war his career continued in Melbourne, Australia, where he spent the rest of his life.

In 1940 he joined the RAF Volunteer Reserve, and it was probably through the Cambridge connection that he found himself, bilingual in German and English as well as having mastery of a handful of other languages, at Bletchley Park. By the end of the war, he was a Wing Commander in the German Air Section, and appointed to lead the TICOM Team No.1 sent to Germany in 1945.

Junior academic colleagues could find him uncongenial, but this meant that Oeser could see through feeble thinking. The *Australian Dictionary of Biography* says he 'appreciated fine art, literature and music, supported progressive education, [and] read voraciously'.

Catching the Fish was just part of it. Team 1 unearthed details of something called the *Forschungsamt*, or research bureau, which turned out to be a separate spying agency working for Reichsmarschall Hermann Göring, who was spying on everything including his own colleagues, and doing his own private piece of signals intelligence into the bargain. And that was not all. In the small hill-town of Ebermannstadt, the team found a secret laboratory codenamed *Feuerstein* (firestone). At *Feuerstein* German scientists had been working on top-secret signals-secrecy engineering projects, including computing equipment and machines for enciphering telephone calls. This was the kind of stuff which needed experts for assessment, and so Alan Turing and Tommy Flowers were both despatched to Ebermannstadt to see how advanced the Germans were.

Into the cold

Near Rosenheim to the east, the team found what might be the most intriguing discovery of the whole TICOM enterprise. Here, captured members of the German Army High Command's own signals intelligence agency disclosed that they had been working on a special form

Members of the TICOM team located German 'Fish' equipment, here being packaged up by prisoners of war to be brought to Britain for analysis.

of Russian non-morse messages. The Germans had invented equipment to tackle this traffic: it was, in the eyes of the Allies, the Russian version of Fish. The German equipment and methodology was priceless. For, as World War II came to a close, the Cold War was springing into life. Working out what the Russians were thinking was the first step in keeping ahead in this new, great game.

Many of the codebreakers – those who had specialized in cryptanalysis, rather than intelligence and interpretation – would be kept on by GCHQ. Some would go on to positions of eminence in the new postwar organization, such as Group Captain Eric Jones, head of Hut 3, who succeeded Sir Edward Travis as the head of GCHQ on the latter's retirement. Other future heads of GCHQ also cut their teeth at Bletchley: Sir Leonard Hooper, who had worked on Italian, and then Japanese, air signals (head of GCHQ from 1965 to 1973); and Sir Arthur Bonsall, who was in the German air section under Josh Cooper (head of GCHQ from 1973 to 1978). But for the majority of staff, the end of hostilities spelt the end of an era.

Sir Eric Jones (1907–86)

When Commander Travis appointed Eric Jones to be head of Hut 3, it was something of a gamble. Jones was an industry manager who had joined the RAF Volunteer Reserve in 1940, so he was not regular air force intelligence, nor a professor, nor a codebreaker. But it was management skills that were needed: in the words of one of the codebreakers, 'administration, organization and authority'. Authority, insofar as it was needed on a formal basis, was conferred with a promotion to the rank of Group Captain, which meant that Jones outranked everyone at Bletchley, including Travis, except John Tiltman (who ended the war as a Brigadier).

A pen-portrait of Jones while head of Hut 3 describes him thus: 'our dignified Group Captain ... always only "Sir" to the rest of us – displayed an impressive manner and a most decorous reserve ... tall, well-built, photogenic of profile with dark brown hair ever precisely in place ... his well-waxed pencil moustache matched by his flawless RAF uniform.'[24] Another pen-portrait, by Stuart Milner-Barry, describes him as 'a genuinely modest man ... liked and trusted by everyone.'

After the war, Jones stayed on rather than returning to industry. He became deputy director of GCHQ in 1950 and succeeded Sir Edward Travis as head of the organization in 1952. He stepped down in 1960; his entry in the *Dictionary of National Biography* says 'some found him ponderous or pompous. Perhaps for this reason, through a lack of empathy between Whitehall mandarins and a man from a quite different background, he was not given further government employment.' Jones turned to growing carnations.

For some, the experience of Bletchley was transformative. Donald Michie and I.J. Good were both dazzled by the science-fiction world of the Newmanry with its futuristic electronic machinery. Michie's career finished up in machine intelligence, and Good commented regularly on its dangers to humanity – a subject which is still live today. (Michie was also close to Alan Turing, whom he accompanied on an abortive mission at the war's end to retrieve some silver ingots. In the autumn of 1940, when everyone feared a German invasion, Turing had converted his cash into specie and buried it, keeping a sketch-map to help locate it. Whether it was because they were using a home-made metal detector

24 Landis Gores, *Ultra: I was there* (2008), p. 65.

or for other reasons, the ingots were never found. Someone within a ten-mile radius of Bletchley is sitting on a fortune.) As with other mathematicians, like Newman, Turing, Good and Welchman, the path of their careers was shaped by their experience at Bletchley.

I.J. (Jack) Good (1916–2009)
Donald Michie (1923–2007)

Good and Michie, with very different backgrounds, were thrown together in 1943 to be Max Newman's first two cryptanalytic assistants. Their time at Bletchley, and particularly their experience of close working with Newman and Alan Turing, led them to make major contributions in the development of artificial intelligence.

Good was born in London to emigré Jewish parents from the Russian partition of Poland. By the age of nine his mathematical abilities were evident – lying ill in bed he had discovered for himself the idea of irrational numbers. He reached Bletchley after doing his PhD in mathematics at Cambridge, and was introduced to Hut 8 by Stuart Milner-Barry whom he had played in a chess tournament only a few days before. (During the match, Good had asked whether Milner-Barry worked on ciphers; Milner-Barry had given the classic response, 'No, my address is Room 47, Foreign Office.')

Michie, rather younger, was recruited straight into the team breaking Tunny from his undergraduate course in classics at Oxford. Soon he was debating with Alan Turing about the possibility of machines being programmed to play a game of chess. After the war, Michie went on to study human

Donald Michie worked on teleprinter ciphers and machinery at Bletchley Park, and later pioneered the study of artificial intelligence.

genetics and anatomy, but he is probably best remembered for his research on machine learning and for establishing the Department of Machine Intelligence at Edinburgh University.

Good's postwar career was also varied: he went to Manchester with Newman, then to GCHQ, and later became a professor of statistics at Virginia Tech. His passionate advocacy of 'Bayesian statistics', then an unfashionable backwater, was grounded in his knowledge that the techniques had worked at Bletchley Park. Good also wrote about the threat of super-intelligent machines, and, after the secrecy which surrounded his wartime work had lifted, drove around in a car with the licence plate '007 IJG'.

In both cases their imaginations were fired by working in the futuristic science-fiction world of electronic computing machines – the Newmanry and Colossus. Michie and Good remained friends for many years; much later, when introducing Good to a lecture audience in 1975, Michie said, 'When I first met Jack, he held out his hand and said "I'm Good." And he has been getting better ever since.'

For others it was a staging-post towards a varied and impressive career: Roy Jenkins, who worked in the Testery, is one example. Asa Briggs, who was called up in 1942 to spend a year as a somewhat unlikely figure in an army uniform, joining Hut 6 under Gordon Welchman in 1943, is another. In some ways, Jenkins and Briggs are mirror-images of each other. Both came from humble origins and had socialist inclinations. Jenkins was a politician who wrote extensively about history, Briggs was a historian who mingled closely with Labour politicians. Both ended up in the House of Lords, both were chancellors of universities and both had reputations as raconteurs and bons viveurs. Posted to

Bletchley, young men like these two would have borne the stigma of 'not doing their bit for the war effort', were it not for the fact that they had joined the ranks. In Jenkins' case, he was a captain; Briggs was a warrant officer 'on a captain's pay', and the uniform was a form of protective clothing.

Roy Jenkins (1920–2003)

To summarize Roy Jenkins's stellar career in a few lines cannot do justice to the man. He was a Labour MP from 1948 to 1976, serving as Minister of Aviation, Home Secretary (twice) and Chancellor of the Exchequer. In government he overcame friction to bring about a series of social and progressive reforms on divorce, homosexuality and abortion. He was President of the European Commission – the only British person to perform the role – from 1977 to 1981. On his return to Britain, with three other leading members of the Labour Party, Jenkins split to establish the new Social Democratic Party, of which he became leader in 1982 after winning a new parliamentary seat in Glasgow. He became a life peer in 1987 and leader of the Liberal Democrats in the House of Lords.

Retirement was a meaningless concept for Jenkins, who remained active in politics but pursued a range of other interests. He was a diligent historical biographer, writing attractive and well-researched biographies of Gladstone and Churchill; having held the high offices of state himself, Jenkins could get under the skin of his subjects and explain the isolation of power. He also wrote his own autobiography: a rare thing for political autobiographies, something which is actually good to read.

Although Roy Jenkins was a brilliant man, he was not considered a very good codebreaker at Bletchley Park. Jenkins admitted as much in his own account of the Bletchley years, confessing that he had been 'seriously off form for several weeks', leading to a demotion of responsibility, albeit mitigated by a promotion to captain in the army.

Asa Briggs (1921–2016)

Asa Briggs joined Bletchley Park via the traditional route, as a Cambridge undergraduate who had played chess with a mathematician in Gordon Welchman's college. As a student he had excelled, picking up degrees in history and economics before he was 20.

But Briggs was surprisingly off-centre when it came to membership of the establishment. He was proud of his northern roots (born in Keighley, and from 1955 a professor at Leeds University) and slightly left-leaning in politics. He was a supporter (and in time chancellor) of Harold Wilson's Open University and served as president of the Workers' Educational Association. As a historian, he specialized in the Victorian era, and he was asked by the BBC to write their history, a project which took over 30 years and amounted to five volumes.

All of this makes Briggs seem dusty and dull, but his wicked sense of humour made him fun as well as intellectually stimulating company. He mingled with the powerful, with Harold Macmillan, James Callaghan and Denis Healey; he refused a safe Labour seat in Parliament, preferring to stay in academia. And in retirement, as Lord Briggs of Lewes, he wrote his own entertaining personal memoir of his years at Bletchley Park.

Being a non-combatant, whether or not in uniform, could come at a price. Years later, Sir Stuart Milner-Barry would say, 'We were hardly at any kind of risk, unlike the Londoners in the Blitz and the inhabitants of other major cities or the fighting services. One could not help sometimes being ashamed of the sheltered life we led.' In the early days of Bletchley, one or two codebreakers argued successfully that they were in the wrong place and left to serve in more conventional ways.

Keith Batey, the husband of Mavis Lever (whose breakthrough had provided the crucial intelligence at Matapan) was himself racked with doubts about doing an intellectual job in relative comfort, and sought a transfer to the front. Perhaps his doubts had been sown by his first landlady, whom he described as 'a horror… She wanted an assurance from the Park that I wasn't a conscientious objector.' Batey changed lodgings. But, once Bletchley had begun to deliver its priceless treasure, combat service was impossible for anyone who had been tainted with the Ultra secret. To be indoctrinated with knowledge of what was going on at Bletchley was instant disqualification for deployment to a battle zone or, indeed, any place where the possibility of capture by the enemy was a significant risk. So Batey had stayed at Bletchley.

Others went back to doing what they had done before the war. As a magnet for those with language skills, Bletchley had its fair share of writers. One was the poet Vernon Watkins for whom Bletchley was more of an interlude – though even for him it could be said that Bletchley transformed his life, since he met his wife Gwen in Block F where they both worked on non-Enigma air force codes. Another

Asa Briggs, a colourful historian, was one of several codebreakers who became well known after the war for a career which had nothing to do with codebreaking.

famous writer was the novelist Angus Wilson, who was notorious at Bletchley for his overt homosexuality, bright bow ties and rather highly-strung nature. Wilson worked on Italian and then Japanese material, and after the war he returned to his normal job in the British Museum's printed books department. (One other writer, in the early days, was Leslie Lambert, who was a Room 40 veteran whose career was at the GC&CS. New recruits to Hut 8 found it something of a shock to hear this distinguished old-school codebreaker's voice, for they recognized it as that of the broadcaster A.J. Alan: under that pen-name Lambert told short stories on the wireless every few months from 1924 until 1940. Alas, Lambert died in service at Bletchley in 1941.)

Vernon Watkins (1906–1967)

Vernon Watkins wanted to be a poet, from the age of five, and that was what he was. His day-job was working for Lloyds Bank, because poetry doesn't pay the bills; but it was his knowledge of modern languages, rather than poetry or banking, which brought him to Bletchley Park in 1942.

Watkins's best friend was Dylan Thomas, another Welsh poet, so it was natural that Watkins would ask Thomas to be his best man in 1944 when Watkins was to marry his fellow-codebreaker Gwen Davies. Unfortunately, Dylan Thomas was Dylan Thomas and he failed to show up at the wedding; somehow the friendship survived. After Bletchley, Watkins returned to South Wales and his poetry, and to Lloyds Bank; the poetry got written in the after-work hours. On his retirement, he described himself as the oldest cashier.

Watkins's reputation has been overshadowed by that of his best friend, but Archbishop Rowan Williams thought that

> Watkins was one of the twentieth century's 'most brilliant and distinctive, yet unjustly neglected, voices.'

For many of the young women recruited as Wrens, WAAFs and ATS, or as civilians under the umbrella of the Foreign Office, the end of the war was the end of a period of drudgery, and demobilization implied a return to traditional social values where a woman's value was measured only in domestic terms. Once again, the uniform could be an advantage: women in the services were entitled to a war medal, but those who had had civilian roles were not. The iniquity of it all was perhaps less obvious, since the War Medal and Defence Medal would only be given automatically to personnel still in uniform after the war ended, and those who had been demobilized needed to apply – and many of those serving at Bletchley did not know about that. It took until 2009 for the UK authorities to do something about it, when a Commemorative Badge issued by GCHQ on behalf of its predecessor was made available to all surviving Bletchley Park veterans.

In his memoirs, Asa Briggs recorded the end of days at Bletchley, punctuated by the news of the atom bomb at Hiroshima.

> *Many of us had left BP before these strange days when relief was mingled with horror. By the end of August [1945] total staff numbers were down from 8,900 to 5,500, and a month after VJ-Day Commander Travis declared that GC&CS was no longer operational. In the spring of 1946 the last person left inside BP, Barbara Abernethy, closed the premises down, locking the huts and the gates....*

The site was closed. Those who continued in secret operations at GCHQ worked for an organization which did not officially exist. The seal of the

Official Secrets Act bound not just those at GCHQ, but everyone who had worked at Bletchley Park and its outstations, to perpetual silence. The achievements of those who worked there, the moments of triumph and despair, were to remain a secret forever.

 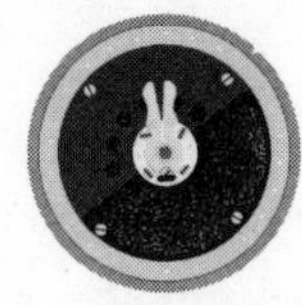 

CHAPTER 10

Official Secrets, Careless Talk

The crucial importance of keeping the secret of Bletchley Park was drummed into the thousands of people recruited to GC&CS during the war years. However minor the role, however distant from the intelligence decisions, however ignorant the staff member was that the place was involved in breaking codes, the process was much the same. Some figure in authority – in the early days, Alastair Denniston himself, later on, an officer or one of the forbidding professors – would give a speech about the importance of secrecy, and from about 1942 onwards the recruit would have to sign the Official Secrets Act. Bletchley Park veterans all recall this induction in a similar way. 'My memory of it is: *never* talk to anyone about what you do, even to your fellow workers, and if you do, on purpose, you may be shot!'[25] The extremity of the penalty for non-adherence to the code of silence echoes through all these memoirs.

The idea is a bit strange, because a person is bound by the Official Secrets Act whether they sign it or not. 'My attention has been drawn to the provisions of Section 2(1), (1a), (2) and 8(2) of the Official Secrets Acts, 1911 and 1920, which are set out below, and I understand the effect of these sections and the serious consequences which may follow

25 Rozanne Colchester, quoted by Tessa Dunlop, *The Bletchley Girls*, p. 102.

any breach of their provisions.'[26] The procedure was one of ceremony – few forgot it who had been through it, and nobody disobeyed it. There was, additionally, a second document called SECRECY, which also had to be signed. It had a list of five commands each beginning DO NOT TALK, and there was practical information about how to answer a question about what you did. The document concluded with the words 'I hereby promise that no word of mine shall betray, however slightly, the great trust placed in me.'

From time to time senior staff had to send out reminders. Bletchley staff were told that bringing a camera into a 'prohibited place' was contrary to the Official Secrets Act. Nigel de Grey sent round a note in September 1944, telling the story of 'a member of this station' who had told a friend 'precisely what her work was, in the course of ordinary conversation.' The friend told another friend and from there the word got back to Bletchley. The staff member who had blabbed was summarily dismissed. It was probably inevitable, with such a large establishment, that there would be security lapses. The implementation of zero tolerance was by Commander Travis in May 1942, in a memo which contains the following:

> *In one instance a member of this organisation employed in responsible duties disclosed their nature within her family circle, thinking no doubt that the secret was safe there, but at the same time flagrantly transgressing the provisions of the Official Secrets Act. What she had disclosed in the family circle was repeated by one of its members in mixed company, actually at a cocktail party, whence it was duly reported to me. …*
>
> *You will yourselves feel that no punishment can be too severe for anyone who endangers the lives of our men and I must insist that you take this matter of security to heart, and hope that I*

26 Official Secrets Act declaration, GC&CS files, National Archives of the United Kingdom.

> *shall not again have to subject you to the indignity of such a warning.*

In the case cited by Travis, the Director of Public Prosecutions had got involved, and proceedings had nearly begun, being forestalled only by the intervention of 'C' himself. The fate of the individual was not disclosed, Travis' account just saying that she had been 'suitably dealt with'. It was an instance of Travis having taken control of Bletchley Park, imposing a starker and more disciplined style on the sometimes unruly codebreakers. Alastair Denniston's approach had been characteristically softer:

> *INDISCREET TALK.*
> *With reference to my memorandum of 7th January, 1942 regarding the suspension from duty of two members of the staff, the order has now been cancelled and the girls have returned to duty. … All members of sections should be warned once again to avoid any talk about their work in the presence of their billetors or any other person.*

It is notable that all these examples of 'indiscreet talk' seem to have women at their centre. It seems unlikely that women were more disposed to talk about their secret work than men, and it is quite clear that the overwhelming majority of staff of both sexes kept their vow of silence diligently, even obsessively. The women involved in these stories may have been singled out and reported on, because it was assumed that they should not be talking whereas talkative men, who equally should have known better, were probably assumed to be authorized to talk.

After VE day in May 1945, when Bletchley Park was sending the codebreakers and other personnel back into civilian life, Travis reminded everyone that the duty of confidentiality was not for the duration of hostilities, but for life: 'The temptation now to "own up" to our friends and family as to what our work has been is a very real and natural one. It must be resisted absolutely.' The *Bletchley District Gazette* wrote hopefully to the Chief of Administration at Bletchley Park on 27 August 1945 to see if 'it would be possible to run a story in our columns regarding Bletchley Park,' but the reply was 'you will know that the Defence Regulations and the Official Secrets Acts, to which we are subject, are still fully effective and we cannot ignore them.'

A privileged few were set to work on official histories. There were many of these. They included an official history of British Sigint, written by Frank Birch (see pages 16–17, Introduction), who had seen it all from the earliest days in 1914; an official history of Hut 3, one of Hut 6, another of Hut 8, a 15-volume history of Naval Sigint (with Birch again taking a major role in drafting), a 19-volume one on Army and Air Force Sigint, and an appreciation (again in several volumes) by Nigel de Grey (see pages 32–3, Chapter 1) of Allied Sigint Policy and Organization. Not one of these documents was for public consumption.

Spies and lies

Perhaps for the majority of Bletchley Park's personnel the ongoing duty of silence was hardly a problem. For many, the job had been just a job, generating little of interest to talk about. Others had had difficulty explaining at home what they had done in the war, which could lead to awkward moments. Ruth Bourne, who operated bombes, was constantly being asked by her mother for details about her war work. 'You got so used to not talking to anyone. Oh yes, I thought. It will be all around Birmingham in five minutes.' So, mother was kept in the dark. Codebreakers mentioned, many years later, how they had not been able to explain to their parents even years later what they had done during the war. Joan Glover is typical: 'Both sets of my family – my family and my husband's – died without knowing, which makes me feel sad,' she said in 2018. 'I could never tell my mother anything.' Even husbands and wives died before their partner's secret could be told, and when the secret did become generally known it left an empty space where there should have been celebration. There were also some strange cases: Joan Unwin had been married to her husband John for 30 years before they realized they had both been stationed at Bletchley during the war.

On the other hand, one former member of Bletchley Park's staff not only told the secret but later in life made a big thing of it. This was John Cairncross, who may be Bletchley Park's most notorious alumnus. After spending a few years in Whitehall, in the foreign office and as private secretary to Lord Hankey, a cabinet minister, Cairncross's language skills saw him posted to Hut 3 for a short period beginning in 1942. By this time Cairncross had been introduced into the ring of upper-crust Cambridge graduates who were working as spies for the Soviet Union. Cairncross himself claimed to have fed decrypts to his controller; he goes further, taking credit for the Red Army's victory at the Battle of the Kursk salient in 1943, which he believes was aided by the intelligence he stole. The claim is doubtful, not simply because wars are won by soldiers not by spies, but because the Soviet Union was regularly given intelligence digests which included sanitized product gleaned from signals intelligence as well as other sources; and, unofficially, Kim Philby sitting in MI6 had a regular flow of output from Bletchley which he was able to mine and send on to Moscow separately. Cairncross's account of his time at Bletchley may simply have been an attempt, late in life, to gain the attention, one way or another, of the British public, to make up for a career which was misdirected and, in many ways, thwarted.

John Cairncross (1913–95)

John Cairncross was never cut out to be a spy. He was a linguist, a literary scholar, and exceptionally clever – and having come first in the Civil Service examinations of 1936 a glittering career in the Foreign Office and diplomatic service beckoned. Yet for some reason – possibly a lifelong desire to be lauded and accepted in a snobbish peer group from which, as a Scot, he seemed to be permanently excluded – he was drawn into the pro-Soviet circle of spies which included Guy Burgess and Anthony Blunt, both of whom he had known at Cambridge.

The Soviets were happy to have Cairncross close to the decision making: in the Foreign Office, as secretary to a Cabinet minister, and at Bletchley Park. After the war, Cairncross went to the Treasury, but his Soviet controllers found this posting less useful, since what they wanted was atomic secrets, to which Cairncross had little access. In fact, Cairncross was rather inept as a spy. One story has him stalling his car in front of a policeman with his Russian controller in the passenger seat and with clearly-marked secret files in plain sight; in panic, Cairncross flooded the engine and could not start the car again.

In 1952, after Burgess fled to Moscow, Cairncross was caught. He lost his job but was never prosecuted, perhaps underscoring his inadequacies as a spy. Rather, his talents seem to have lain in literary criticism. His self-serving account – a last attempt to acquire elusive stardom – of his career at Bletchley was published posthumously in 1997, triggering a row about authorship with the spy writer Rupert Allason. Cairncross was nothing if not controversial.

Cairncross's autobiography was issued in 1997, by which time the Bletchley Park secret was well out in the open. The story of its exposure is in some ways curious, since the British authorities had no desire to disclose what Bletchley Park had done, for that would risk explaining that there was an institution called GCHQ, which was not really supposed to exist, which had a huge budget which would not easily be explained, and which carried on activities which British governments did not want anyone to know about. Yet, by the mid-1970s, the official secret of Bletchley had become too big for containment.

Spilling the beans

A handful of beans had been spilled in the postwar years, but by the early 1970s a handful was turning into a sackful. The broadcaster Malcolm Muggeridge had served with MI6 and was in on the secret: his autobiography, published in 1973, devotes several pages to it. 'Cracked cipher material was, indeed, the staple product of MI6, and provided the basis for most of its effective activities.... The establishment which produced this precious material was located at Bletchley, in a manor house in which I spent some days familiarizing myself with the place, its staff, its output and manner of working.' Muggeridge was not alone. Others, who had done their time at Bletchley and were approaching retirement age in the 1970s, wanted to write their memoirs too. GCHQ

John Cairncross, who spied on the spies.

repeatedly said 'No' when asked for permission to publish particulars of Bletchley Park.

Beyond the confines of the British Isles it was another story. Following small revelations in Poland and France, none other than Gustave Bertrand, who by the early 1970s was a retired General of Brigade, having risen in the postwar French intelligence service, decided to write his own account of the Enigma challenge and the work he had done with the Poles and the British during the 1930s and 1940s. Bletchley Park itself was not mentioned, but the idea was out. A fluster developed

Enigma revelations (1945–1979)

1945	Articles in *Time* and *Life* magazines in the United States reveal that Allies had broken German and Japanese codes during the war.
1967	Polish historian Władysław Kozaczuk reveals that Polish codebreakers had broken the Enigma machine before World War II – but in Polish and in Poland.
1969-1973	A handful of minor passages by Malcolm Muggeridge in book reviews and biographical writings say that the British broke codes at Bletchley Park – but he writes about playing rounders on the lawn, not Enigma machines.
1972	Gustave Bertrand's book *Enigma* breaks the story of Enigma in the West – without mentioning Bletchley Park.
1974	*The Ultra Secret*, by F.W. Winterbotham, brings the story of Bletchley Park into the open.
1979	Volume I of the official history, *British Intelligence in the Second World War*, is published.

in Whitehall, with various Bletchley veterans penning memos criticizing Bertrand's book – but a book in French with a limited print run did not amount to a sensation in Britain, at least not yet. Nevertheless, historians were on the case, and the story of secret intelligence gleaned from coded signals was too spicy to leave alone.

Officials and history

Sooner or later the truth would leak out from this high-pressure canister of secrecy, and in 1974 the lid blew right off. The British 'D-Notice Committee' (which issues official 'requests' to the media not to publish on national security grounds) got wind of a new book, to be published in America by a British journalist, which would reveal the best-kept secret of World War II. Because its publication was going to be in the United States, no D-Notice could stop it. The only thing was to issue some sort of partial, authorized, and (with luck) diversionary story first.

Group Captain Frederick Winterbotham, who had served with distinction in Air Intelligence during the war, was not only an insider but he was a professional spy, now on the retired list. He went through the proper channels, discussing his proposal with Admiral Farnhill, the chairman of the D-Notice Committee, his predecessor (and World War II naval intelligence officer) Admiral Denning, and the head of GCHQ, Sir Joseph Hooper (himself a veteran of Bletchley Park's Air Section). By 1974 there was a cautious no-action comment from Farnhill, and Winterbotham's publishers went ahead. The book, *The Ultra Secret*, was thus the semi-official story, and it sold over four million copies. Packed with sensational detail – much of it inaccurate, since Winterbotham had written largely from memory, without access to official records, and without detailed technical knowledge of exactly what had been done in many sections at Bletchley – it was a runaway breathless disclosure, and no distraction at all, notwithstanding that Winterbotham had restricted himself to the distribution and application of Bletchley Park's intelligence product, and not to cover the technicalities of codebreaking (which he would have been ill-equipped to do).

Frederick Winterbotham (1897–1990)

Winterbotham's fame derives from his bestselling book, *The Ultra Secret*, which brought the story of Bletchley Park and its influence on the course of World War II to an astonished public in the mid-1970s. Winterbotham went on to write more about his life, with two more books, which show that there was a lot more to him than his best-known role, that of exposer of secrets, might suggest.

In World War I, Winterbotham joined the cavalry, switching to the Royal Flying Corps in 1916. He was shot down in a dog-fight over Passchendaele and spent the rest of the war as a prisoner, and he learned German. On his release, he studied law at Oxford and then went into agriculture.

In 1929, he was recruited by MI6 to their newly-fledged air intelligence section, and he spent much of the 1930s in Germany, pretending to be a Nazi sympathizer while checking out the latest developments in aircraft technology and resources. He helped pioneer high-altitude photo-reconnaissance, and in 1940 he joined Bletchley Park as an air intelligence officer. His principal achievement there, as explained in detail in *The Ultra Secret*, was to establish the system of Special Liaison Units located with field commanders to receive and deliver Ultra intelligence. He was promoted to Group Captain and received a CBE.

For most people that would have been a full enough CV, but Winterbotham's reputation relies on *The Ultra Secret*. The tale of how that book came to be published is itself a drama; its sequel runs on, since it contains many stories, which not only established the reputation of Bletchley Park but planted a number of enduring myths and fantasies which, somehow, are hard to correct.

With the revelations, people could at last tell their loved ones that they had not, after all, been completely useless in Britain's hour of need. Computer historian Brian Randell wrote to Alan Turing's mother – herself then 94 years old – on 27 November 1975, to say that 'the Government have recently made an official release of information which contains an explicit recognition of the importance of your son's work ... a book has recently been published ... which ... credits your son as being the main person involved in the breaking of one of the most important German codes, the Enigma Code, and thus implies that his work was of vital importance to the outcome of World War II.'

The floodgates were open, the BBC ran a television series on the 'secret war', and German decrypts were released to the National Archives. Jenny Conduit, a Wren who had been stationed at Stanmore, explained how 'when F.W. Winterbotham's book *The Ultra Secret* was published in 1974 and the story exploded on television and in the newspapers I found that I was unable to stop chattering about it for days. All this knowledge with which I had expected to go to the grave came bubbling up to the surface.' That was, as far as the British authorities were concerned, something of a problem – the codebreakers wanted to chatter, and the bubbling was a symptom experienced by everyone, not just former Wrens. By 1978 there were so many who wanted to write their memoirs that there was a parliamentary question, to which the Foreign Secretary responded:

> **Dr. Owen** ... *gave the following information: The release of Enigma/Ultra records to the Public Record Office has understandably caused those who worked on or used this material and who have maintained the undertakings of reticence which they gave at the time to ask where they now stand.... [They] are now absolved from them to the limited extent that they may now disclose the fact that they worked on or used material based on intercepted messages of the enemy armed forces.... Other information may not be disclosed.... As the Prime Minister told*

the hon. Member for Melton (Mr. Latham) on 30th November, the preparation of an Official History of Intelligence in World War II is well advanced.

Perhaps the official history would answer the questions people had, but it seemed that the gag was still in place as regards what people had actually done at Bletchley Park, even though the war had been over for more than 30 years.

Gordon Welchman's story

The first volume of the official history came out in 1979. Its chief editor was Professor F.H. Hinsley, himself a veteran of Bletchley Park and now Master of St John's College, Cambridge. Over the coming years there would be five more volumes (counting parts one and two of volume three, each of which is a big book) with a wealth of detail – but little technical information on codebreaking, even though the authors drew extensively on the product of Bletchley Park. Much of the source-material remained secret. This must have hampered the authors, since volume one contained some gross errors, especially in its absurd mis-telling of the Enigma backstory and the contribution of the Polish codebreakers.

F.H. (Harry) Hinsley (1918–98)

Harry Hinsley came from humble origins to read history at Cambridge University. He was a third-year undergraduate when war broke out, yet was summoned for the customary interview with Alastair Denniston and soon found himself in Hut 4 doing traffic analysis. When the British were withdrawing from Norway in June 1940, his advice to the Admiralty that the German cruisers *Gneisenau* and *Scharnhorst* were on their way to intercept British ships was ignored. Not a surprising result, given that Hinsley was 21 years old. But he was right. The British aircraft carrier HMS *Glorious* was sunk on 8 June. Thereafter, his deductions carried rather more weight. Some while later, a query from the Home Fleet about the source of some intelligence was answered curtly with the one word 'Hinsley'. That was enough.

Hinsley married Hilary Brett-Smith, who was from Somerville College, Oxford, and worked in Hut 8. After the war, Hinsley received an OBE and began a distinguished career as historian and scholar of International Relations. He became known in Cambridge for his trademark outdoor gear: three-piece suit, plastic mac and black beret, worn in all seasons including the hottest summers. His multi-volume official history, *British Intelligence in the Second World War*, published in instalments from 1979 to 1990 (not to mention an abridged edition and a top-up volume issued after the main series to bring it up to date), remains a key reference work on the topic. Hinsley was knighted in 1985.

Bletchley Park's ex-codebreakers could be forgiven for being rather confused by Dr Owen's pronouncement, assuming that they were aware of it. One could hardly say that Frederick Winterbotham had stuck to the principle of just admitting 'I was there' – he had done a whole lot more than that, explaining in great detail the system of Special Liaison Units which he had established for the distribution of Ultra intelligence, giving particulars of the work done at Bletchley to decipher Enigma, and more. Other memoirs and histories were in similar vein, though perhaps most focused on the characters encountered at the Park, and the achievements based on the intelligence delivered, rather than the technical specificities of bombe machines and the like. One exception was the memoir of Gordon Welchman, who was eager to set out the astonishing achievement of the bombe. Aged 75 and now based in the United States, and with the Enigma machine consigned to antiquity, Welchman thought he was free to explain, in a book called *The Hut Six Story*. He later recalled:

> *I seemed to have a very special responsibility in that I was the only person alive with inside knowledge of a very telling episode in cryptologic history .... But in April 1982, when the book had just been published, my troubles began. I was interviewed by special agents for having allegedly disclosed information about wartime cryptanalysis that is still regarded as classified in England .... My security badge was taken away .... So, 42 years after Hut 6 achieved its first success ... I suddenly found myself branded as a security risk.*

If losing his (United States) security clearance was a blow, the British were about to rub salt into Gordon Welchman's wounds. In July 1985, Welchman went into print again, this time to present a corrected version of the Enigma story, to counter the errors in the official history. His article was cleared by the D-Notice Committee, but that didn't seem to count. The same month, Sir Peter Marychurch, the head of GCHQ, wrote a stinging report, phrased as if Welchman was an errant sixth-former: 'We do not expect outsiders to show any great sense of responsibility in what they publish, but you can perhaps understand that it is a bitter blow to us, as well as a disastrous example to others, when valued ex-colleagues decide to let us down.'

The absurdity of it – especially as the existence of GCHQ was now publicly acknowledged – did not go unremarked. Sir Stuart Milner-Barry (see pages 110–11, Chapter 4) went on the counter-attack: 'To suppose that the battles which we had to wage before the birth of the first electronic computer (which must seem to present-day cryptanalysts rather like fighting with bows and arrows) could be relevant to security now is just not credible.' But 1985 was the last year of Gordon Welchman's life, and to have it come to an end in this distressing way, while he should have been honoured as one of the geniuses of Bletchley, is genuinely tragic.

These days GCHQ has come out of the shadows, a vast amount of material (not all of it flattering) has been released to the National Archives, and the achievements of Bletchley Park are rightly celebrated by the authorities as well as by the nation as a whole. As part of its centenary celebrations in 2019, GCHQ announced plans for a new authorized history of the agency, and to give 'as many source documents from the history as we can to the National Archives, alongside our continued programme of releasing previously secret documents from our past.' So there may be further secrets to discover, and still more to learn about the codebreakers of Bletchley Park.

Further Reading

Before and after Bletchley Park

Inside Room 40 by Paul Gannon (Ian Allan Publishing, 2010)

GCHQ by Richard J Aldrich (HarperCollins, 2010)

Behind the Enigma: The Authorised History of GCHQ, Britain's Secret Cyber Intelligence Agency by John Ferris (Bloomsbury, 2020)

Bletchley Park, and its people

The Secrets of Station X by Michael Smith (Biteback Publishing, 2011)

Bletchley Park People by Marion Hill (The History Press, 2004)

The Bletchley Girls by Tessa Dunlop (Hodder & Stoughton, 2015)

The Secret Life of Bletchley Park by Sinclair McKay (Aurum Press, 2010)

The Ultra Americans by Thomas Parrish (Stein & Day, 1986)

Enigma and Colossus

X, Y and Z – the real story of how Enigma was broken by Dermot Turing (The History Press, 2018)

The Hut Six Story by Gordon Welchman (M & M Baldwin, 2011)

Colossus – the secrets of Bletchley Park's codebreaking computers by B. Jack Copeland (Oxford University Press, 2006)

Biographies

Prof – Alan Turing decoded by Dermot Turing (Pavilion, 2015)

Dilly – the man who broke Enigmas by Mavis Batey (Biteback Publishing, 2009)

Alastair Denniston: Code-breaking from Room 40 to Berkeley Street and the birth of GCHQ by Joel Greenberg (Frontline Books, 2017)

The Last Cambridge Spy – John Cairncross, Bletchley Codebreaker and Soviet Double-agent by Chris Smith (The History Press, 2019)

Index